ज्योतिष लय ब्रह्माण्ड की बहती सरित समान।
उद्‌गम पर अध्यात्म है संगम पर विज्ञान।।

Jyotish Laya Brahmand ki Bahati Sarit Saman
Udgam Par Adhyatam Hai Sangam Par Vigyan

Astrology

(Third Eye of Vedas)

Dr. Gopal Das Neeraj
Dr. Arastu Prabhakar

FUSION BOOKS

Publisher	:	**Fusion Books** X-30, Okhla Industrial Area, Phase-II New Delhi-110020
Phone	:	011- 40712200
E-mail	:	wecare@diamondbooks.in
Website	:	www.diamondbooks.in
Edition	:	2025
Printed by	:	Repro (India)

Astrology (Third Eye of Vedas)
Dr. Gopal Das Neeraj, Dr. Arastu Prabhakar

Contents

INTRODUCTION

Astrology is called the third eye of Vedas. It is the permutation and combination of light. The entire universe is governed by the law of energy. This energy in the form of light through the medium of planets governs, controls and directs our activities till our death. The pseudo intellectuals who brand astrology a hoax, do not know even the basic principles of astrology. It is the music of the cosmos—

Jyotish Laya Brahmand ki Bahati Sarit Saman
Udgam Par Adhyatam Hai Sangam Par Vigyan

Each & every particle of the universe vibrates due to this music. There are various methods prevailing in India to judge the nativity viz. *Parasari, Siddhanta Gemini, Yavan, Surya Siddhanta* etc. It is not possible for an astrologer to get mastery over a particular *Siddhant* in a short span of life. It is imperative to mention here the work of Late K. S. Krishna Murti, which is popularly known as *Krishnamurti Padhati* or K. P. The work of Late Krishnamurti is really an innovation in the field of astrology in India. The present book comprises many chapters on K. P. In India to understand K.P. and its application in day to day activities, please refer 'Times Prashna Jyotish' By Dr. Arastu Prabhakar.

All the chapters included in this book are the outcome of the research carried out over a decade and every chapter includes informative contents which might be quite useful to readers. The book is an effort to set astrology free from the clutches of orthodoxy, pendantism, traditionalism and all set to reflect the principles of the universe with logical explanation. The book opens new vistas for research-minded scholars to carry out further research in the field of astrology.

Padam Shree Dr. Gopal Das Neeraj &
Dr. Arastu Prabhakar

TRANSIT—
THE PERPETUATION OF EVENTS

The zodiac is always moving. The effects of the planets are always in accordance with the positions they get during the movement of the zodiac. The nativity is studied with the positions of the planets as they occupy at the time of birth. However the actions, thoughts etc. are governed and influenced more or less by the transiting planets. It has been found that planet in transition gives predominantly the effects if the *dasa* or *antardasa* operating coincides with the transiting planets. Transiting planets fail to give results if *dasa* or *antardasa* operating does not match with the transiting planets.

In order to understand the strength of the planet to produce effects, the study of *prastarashtak varga* is taken into account. Good or bad result of any transiting planet cannot be known without the study of *prastarashtak varga.* The degree of results is also better known from the *prastarashtak varga.* The *prastarashtak charka* also reveals the timing of the events. The *kaksha siddhanta* of *prastarashtak varga* of *asthak varga* system of prediction is of immense value.

Retrogression of Planets

Although the planets move in the same direction round the sun, the apparent motion as seen from the earth is not always in the same direction. They sometimes appear to move also in the backward direction. In astrology the retrograde planets are considered to be near to the earth than their actual distance when they are in direct motion. Therefore, the planets like Saturn, Jupiter which have long stay in a particular sign, influence the native according to their nature. Saturn, being delaying and sluggish planet, tends to delay the matter if it is in retrogression. Similarly, Jupiter tends to materialise the event as soon as it becomes retrogressive.

Study of Transiting Planets either from Ascendant or the Moon

All the classical literature of astrology advocates the study of transit, pertaining to the natal position of the Moon. However, if better results are to be obtained then transition should be studied in respect to ascendant.

Let Us Discusss a few Case Studies

1. DOB : 30.04.1970
   TOB : 6.55 a.m.
   POB : Allahabad

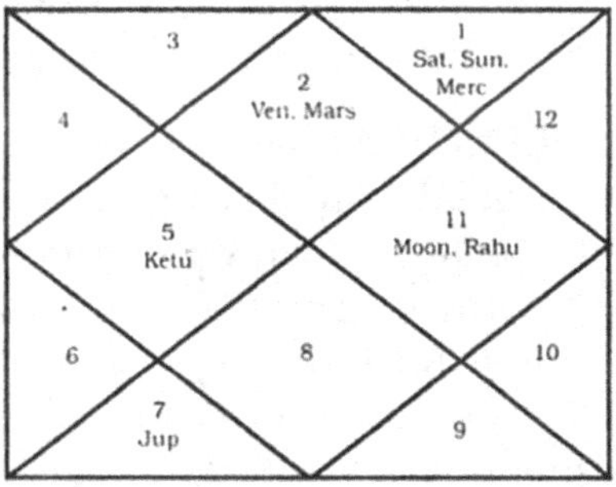

The native was selected for a government job on June 2001. She was not allowed to join the service due to some conditions as imposed by the selection authorities. She was running Jupiter *mahadasa* and Moon *antardasa*. What was the reason of delay and disappointment? Saturn, the *yogakaraka* for Taurus nativity in transition was in ascendant and became retrograde in mid June 2001. Saturn is also the lord of the tenth house and also aspecting the tenth house from ascendant. The retrograde Saturn delayed her appointment. Though *mahadasa* of the native was that of the Jupiter. As soon as Jupiter got retrogression the situation got improved and on 12-11-01 she finally got the appointment letter. At this time Venus was in the sixth house (house of service) in its own *mooltrikona* sign. *Prastarashtak varga* reveals very good position of *dasa nath* and *bhukti nath*. As per natal position Jupiter got more than 4 *bindus* similarly the moon got more than 4 *bindus*. Jupiter in sign Gemini got 5 *bindus*.

Note: 1. The planets which have more than five *bindus* are always auspicious. Below five *bindus* are always related with hurdles, impediments and all kinds of mishappenings.

2. She met an accident on 16th Feb 2001. At this time she was running Jupiter *mahadasa* and Sun *antardasa*. On this fateful day Jupiter being the lord of the 8th house was placed in ascendant and was passing through the *kaksha* of Mars (1s- 8d-6m). Here it is to be noted that Mars is the significator of accidents, fire, motor etc. Mars is also the lord of the 12th house, the house of hospitals etc. Therefore, Jupiter becomes

doubly lethal, one due to lordship over the eighth house simultaneously passing through the *kaksha* of 12th lord, i.e. Mars.

Note: It may be inferred that the placement of the eighth lord in transit in ascendant may be dangerous if *mahadasa* of the said planet is also operating.

Case Study 2:

DOB : 09.06.1968
TOB : 10:20 p.m.
POB : Agra

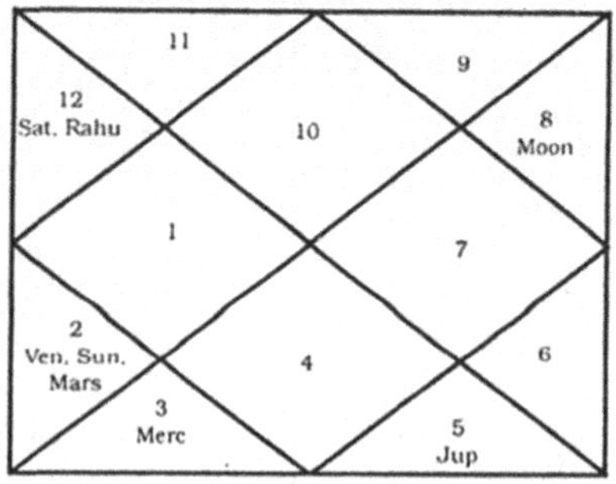

1. The native was running Ketu *mahadasa* and Saturn *antardasa* from 25th Dec. 2000 to 2nd Feb 2002.

Saturn in transit was in Taurus sign, i.e. in the fifth house from ascendant or in the seventh house from Moon. His wife met an accident on 16th Feb 2001 and got fracture in her left ankle. Since, Saturn in transit was placed to the seventh to Moon. The seventh house denotes marriage as well as marriage partner and also friends, partners etc. Saturn was placed fifth to ascendant. Saturn in transit in Taurus sign was also aspecting the seventh house of the native. Since, Saturn is natural malefic but ascendant lord too. Even then Saturn can not shed off its malefic nature completely.

2. The native himself was transferred in peculiar circumstances on 5th June 2001 from the place where he was working for the last seven years. Since the seventh house also denotes business partner or those whom you are dealing with. Saturn from the fifth house in transit severed the relations of the native with his employers because Saturn was aspecting the seventh house coincided with Saturn *antardasa* in Ketu *mahadasa*.

Case Study 3:

DOB : 20.05.1974
TOB : 11:20 p.m.
POB : Agra

1. The native was running Mars *mahadasa* and Saturn *antardasa* from 4th Dec 2000 to 13 Jan 2001. Mars and Saturn both have given 4 *bindus* in their respective *prastarashtak varga*. Both are natural malefic. Saturn is ascendant lord, while Mars is lord of the eleventh house.

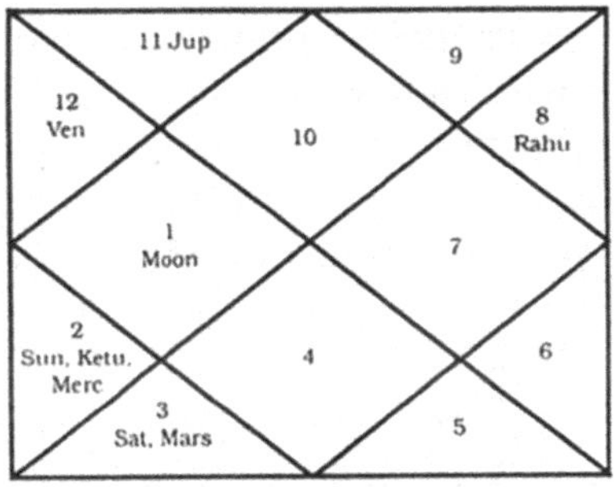

The *dasa* and *antardasa* did not give any tangible results to the native till Oct 2001. In Oct 2001 Mars transited Capricorn sign which is said to be exalted place for Mars. Mars too gave 5 *bindus* in its *prastarashtak varga* in Capricorn sign. Mars being the lord of the eleventh house was exalting during Oct 2001 (not exact dates), therefore Saturn became retrograde, thus more powerful. Even then Mars gave not only liquid assets but also properties to the native because *mahadasa* was that of Mars.

2. Mars *mahadasa* and Mercury *antardasa* started from 13th Jan 2002. Mercury during its stay in Capricorn sign too gave auspicious results. Mars transited Pisces sign on 12th Jan and gave five *bindus* in Pisces sign in its *prastarashtak varga*. On 16th or 17th Jan 2002 the native earned huge money.

Note: Lord of the ninth house, if passes through ascendant, coinciding with either *mahadasa* or *antardasa* gives very auspicious results provided transiting planets be friendly to the ascendant sign.

Case Study 4:

DOB : 02.08.1966
TOB : 16.30
POB : Agra

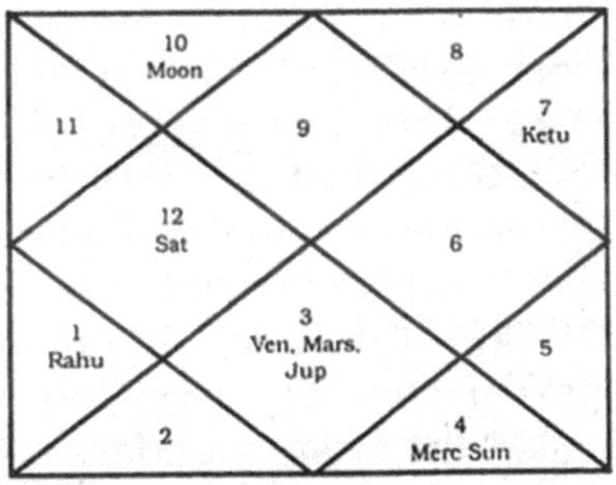

The native is running Jupiter *mahadasa* and Mars *antardasa* from 17th Aug 2001 to 24th July 2002. Mars in transit in Capricorn sign started manifesting its results. Mars being the significator of land properties allruded her to enter into land selling and purchasing. Mars in Meen Sign which happens to be in the fourth house from ascendant represents land properties that boosted her efforts and she finalized big deals right form Oct 2001 to 10 Feb 2002.

Case Study 5:

DOB : 03.07.1972
TOB : 6.50 a.m.
POB : Lucknow

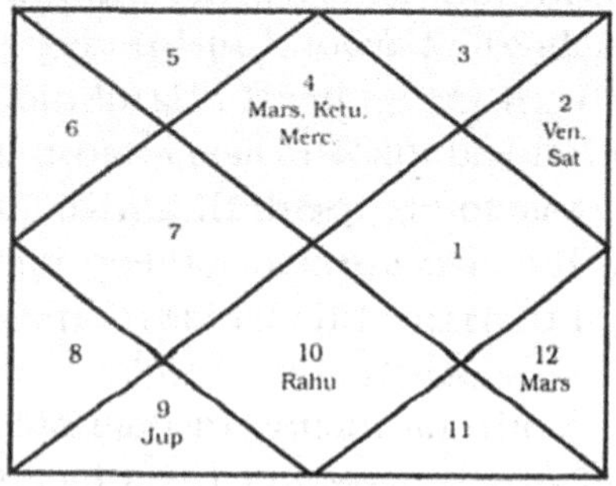

The native was working as a teacher in a government college in Lucknow. She was much anxious to be transferred to another place. She was transferred to her desired place and took the charge on 30 July 2001. At that time she was running Mercury *mahadasa* and Rahu *antardasa*. Mercury, during 9th July 2001 to 28th July 2001, was in Gemini sign in transit, i.e. in the 12th house from ascendant. Mercury is also the ruler of the third house. Both the houses, i.e. the third and the twelfth represent change of place. Rahu was also in Gemini sign during this period. Jupiter transited Gemini sign on 18th June 2001. She transferred when she was running Mercury *mahadasa*, Rahu *antardasa* and Jupiter *pratyantara dasa*.

This period ran form 16th May 2001 to 17th Sept 2001. Jupiter, the lord of the sixth house (house of service), and the ninth one (Journey), was stationed in the 12th house in transit from ascendant. The houses which signify transfer or change of place were strongly ruled by Mercury and Jupiter. Since the transfer is related to service, therefore, the final role was played by Jupiter due to its rulership over the sixth and ninth houses and occupancy over 12th house. She joined new place of service on 30th July 2001 when Mercury, the *Dasanath*, transited Cancer sign, i.e. ascendant of the native. Ascendant itself is called the basic foundation of life. The Mercury in transit in Cancer sign gave new start of life in new circumstances.

Note: Whenever the lord of the fourth house transits either the twelfth or the third house from ascendant, the native is likely to change the place if *mahadasa* or *antardasa* of the said planet is in force. If the lord of 9th house too goes to the twelfth house in transit, the native is likely to leave his or her present place of living.

DETERMINATION OF SUCCESS AND FAILURE IN CAREER

It is seen in all walks of life that some persons are more successful in their life, while most are bereft of any success and wander pillar to post in search of a stable job or profession. Although many persons belong to rich families, yet success does not bestow on them. It has also been noticed in many cases that natives have some *rajyoga* in their horoscopes but they are deprived of any benefit.

Astrological explorations in this direction reveal the fact that success or failure largely depends on one's inclination towards one's field of action. In other words, it can be stated if one's nature or natural tendencies are synchronizing with one's field of action then one's success is assured.

For example, a person having adventurous tendencies is employed in the bank, what will be the result. The person simply carries out the service as a means to make both ends meet. He cannot take this service as a mission because his tendencies are entirely different from his job. His tendencies compel him to be risk seeker, while his job in the bank requires attention and accuracy where any error may lead to total chaos in terms of cash. Similarly, a person having philosophical tendencies is employed in either police or military. Can he be a good officer? Never, because his tendencies compel him to be a philanthropist, while service in force requires some sort of brutality.

It is, therefore, necessary to answer the question of one's success or failure, in either job or profession, keeping in mind his tendencies—explicit or implicit. Predictions about success or failure, in either job or profession, simply made on the configuration of planets, have been found in many cases to be incorrect. Experiences of Indian saints and sages reveal the fact when somebody desires something with his sole devotion or desire, came out from the lowest strata of soul, it is fulfilled. Why is it so?

Man is considered to be a part of the universe when there are some sorts of vibrations at his soul level, the universe also vibrates simultaneously and gives rise to the same vibrations as required by man.

There is a purpose of creation of the universe. It is the purpose of the Almighty or unmoved mover or ultimate energy to provide happiness to each and every individual of the universe. Why do they then suffer? Suffering is not caused by God. Sufferings are caused by society which is the creation of men. Every society is limited in its scope. According to its limitations, society exists for general happiness of mankind in which someone has to suffer at the cost of others. A general destiny is formed by God but its local destiny is formed by society. When a particular horoscope promises to a native that he will have many elephants and will be equal to the rank of a king. What does it mean? In India even a person having good service or profession is equal to king, because a large section of society in India is wallowing in poverty and where it is difficult for a person to make both ends meet. In that sense a person with good service is equal to king.

In a horoscope the 10th house is related with profession, while the 6th house is related with service. The 3rd house denotes tendencies. Therefore, on the basis of above explanation it is important to discuss houses viz. 3rd and 6th for service and the 3rd and 10th houses for profession.

The third house not only represents mental characteristics but also shows devotion and courage which are required ahead in life. The third house determines the direction in which energy of a native flows. It is the 6th to 10th house and 10th to 6th house as far as service is concerned, it denotes capacity, mental tendencies and degree of courage through which a native does well in service. As far as profession is concerned the third house denotes hurdles, disputes, which are a necessary part of a profession. Thus the 3rd house also shows accumulated *karmas* of the previous life because it is just opposited to the 9th house. Thus the 3rd house prepares the native according to his tendencies and generates energy through which the native thrives well in his life. The various ancient classical texts have mentioned various rules for the determination of profession. But determination of either profession or service does not promise that the native will rise high in his career. It is simply his devotion, courage and his previous accumulated deeds that determine his success in life.

Example 1:

This chart belongs to former prime minister Shri Atal Behari Vajpayee. Here the 3rd house is occupied by Jupiter, Sun and Mercury. *Budh Aditya Yoga* in the third house results in cultivation of knowledge of various subjects. The placement of Jupiter and aspect of Saturn on the third house makes him philosophical bent of mind. Two planets viz. Jupiter and Saturn also make him philosopher but Saturn also makes him materialistic. Therefore, such persons dwell between philosophical and materialistic matter. However, materialistic tendencies are reduced to a greater extent. Saturn's aspect over the third house makes him duty-conscious and placement of Jupiter in the third house creates a urge for the betterment of mankind.

He has been in politics for the last fifty years. Politics is neither considered a profession nor service because it is simple *seva* (service) for the people of India. The lord of the 6th house, Jupiter, is placed in the third house denoting a personality craving for the welfare of people because the 6th house is considered to be the house of *shudras*, i.e. masses and the placement of the divine planet viz. Jupiter clearly indicates high association with the masses. He elevated to the post of prime minister because the 10th house is aspected by *Rajyog karaka* Saturn. Thus it is concluded that love for people, selfless service and single minded devotion to the causes of the people, destiny played the way for him. From where he could serve the people of India more efficiently.

Born on 25.12.1924 at 2.30 a.m. at Gwalior.

Balance of *Budh mahadasa* at the time of birth - 10Y 1M 24D

Birth Chart

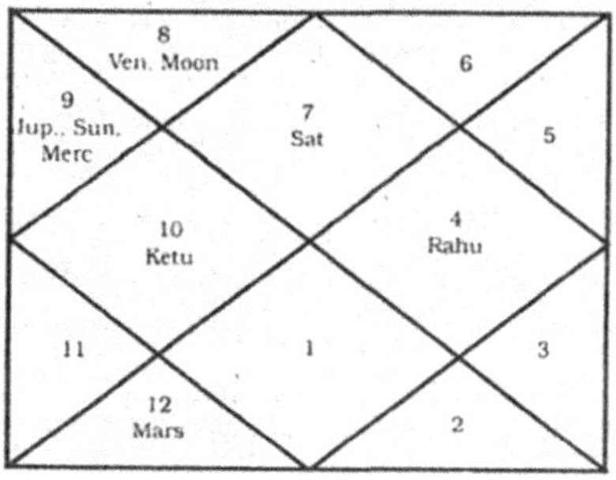

Example 2:

Born on 31.03.1940 at 11 p.m. at Agra
Balance of Sun *mahadasa* at birth - 4Y 7M 24D

Birth Chart

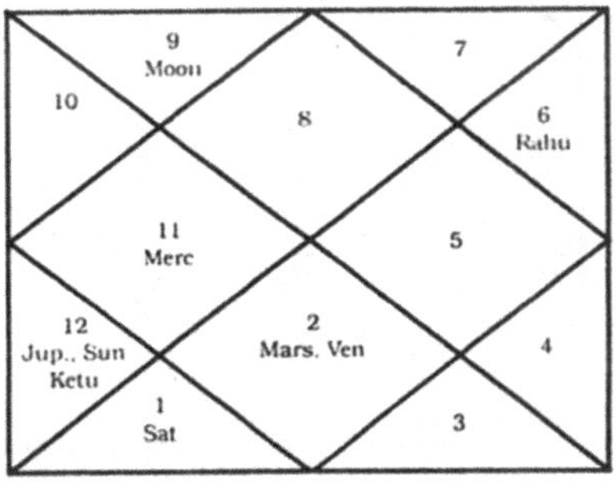

Navamsa

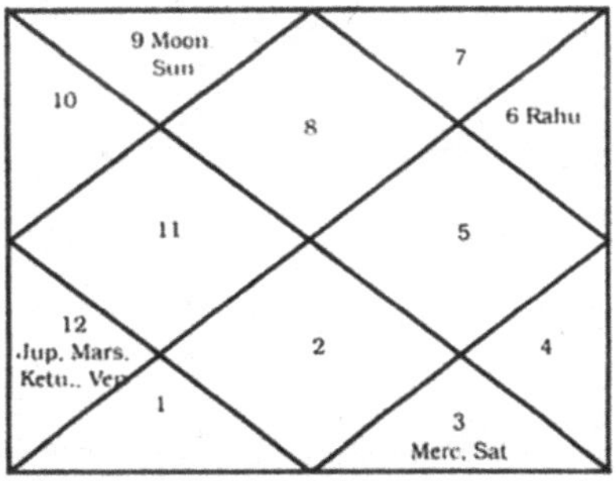

This chart belongs to a highly successful lady. She is practical, generous, calculative and knows well how to take right decision at the right time. The third house lord is debilitated in the 6th house showing poor performance in service. Saturn's aspect over the third house makes her courageous but it has also been seen that the third house associated with Saturn fills with a kind of fear. She is suffering with such a fear. 10th lord Sun is associated with Jupiter. Although she is in service of no importance, yet her association with other activities can be discerned with the 10th house as she is associated with many social institutions where her activities are highly acclaimed. Conjunction of the Sun and Jupiter resulted in the activation of Jupiter which associated her to such institutions as signified by Saturn. She is associated with institutions like Sarvodya, charitable trust, etc. Although Sun in the fifth house is not at all desirable, yet due to the influence of Jupiter she got many awards. The lord of the third house aspects Jupiter in *navamsa* making her plodding and long for none.

Example 3:

Born on 08.10.1925 at 4.20 a.m. at Moradabad.
Balance of Mars *mahadasa* at birth — 3Y 1M 9D

Birth Chart

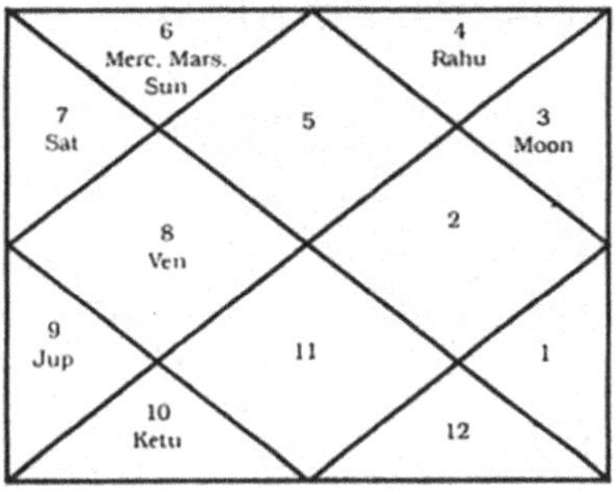

Navamsa

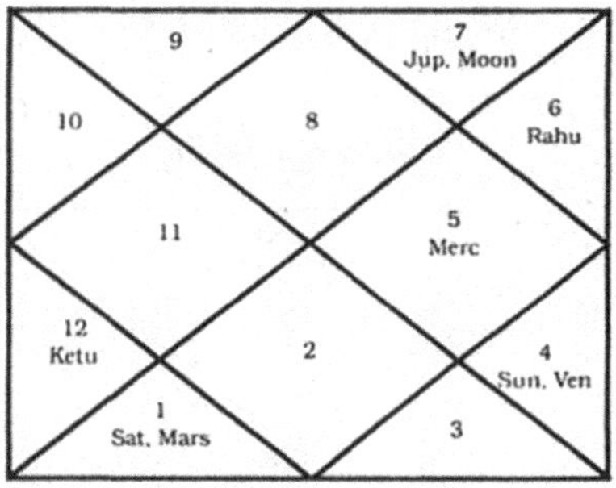

This chart belongs to a retired additional district Judge. The third house is occupied by the exalted Saturn which makes him not only duty-conscious but also have a spirit of justice. The 6th house lord being Saturn clearly indicates service in the department pertaining with disputes. Further in *navams* a Mars-Saturn conjunction in the sixth house clearly indicates service in judiciary. It is further strengthened by the aspect of Jupiter over the sixth house. Jupiter's placement in the 5th house and Saturn's aspect on Jupiter makes him thinker and such aspect enables him to think every matter in its proper perspective and in depth. Saturn and Jupiter make him to give verdict over disputes because Jupiter is lawyer and Saturn is criminal as both planets afflicting, turned him towards judiciary. He would have elevated further had he been capable of manipulation.

He liked to be in isolation and cut-off himself from the mainstream of judiciary.

In natal chart the lord of the 6th and 7th houses is exalted in the third house denoting good rise in service. Further the third house's lord is placed in the 6th house in conjunction with Mars. Sat-Mars Saturn conjunction is not conducive but Jupiter's aspect over the 6th house generates a good *yoga* which moulded his thinking and directed his energy towards judiciary.

Example 4:

Born on 03.03.1943 at 2.15 a.m. at Dhar (M.P.)
Balance of Venus *mahadasa* at birth - 5Y 7M 24D.

Birth Chart

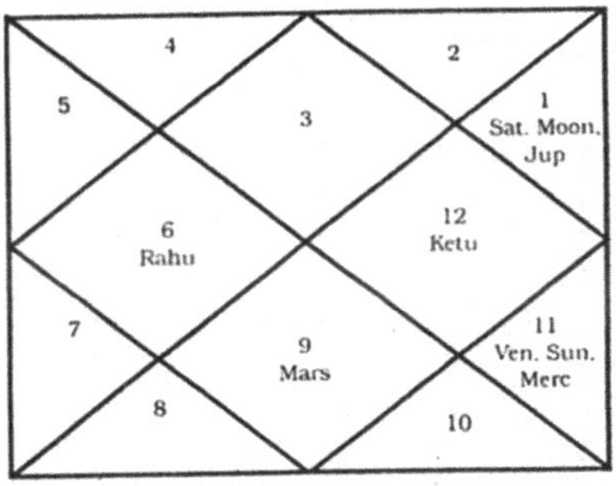

Navamsa

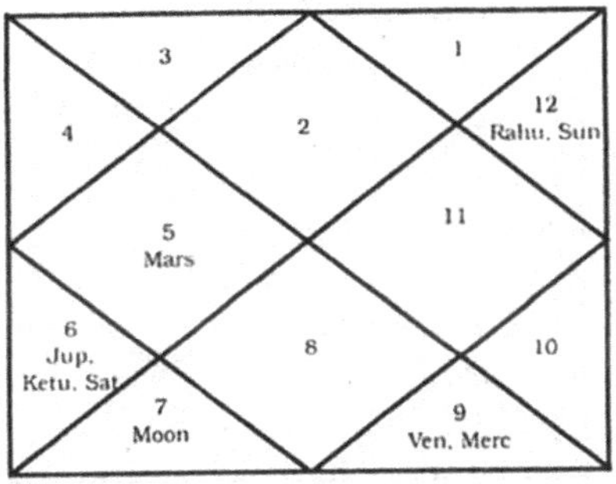

The third house lord is placed in the 9th house along with Venus and Mercury. Sun-Mercury conjunction forms *Budh-Aditya Yoga* making him intelligent and learned. The 3rd house is aspected by the Sun making him courageous, adventurous and a soul ready to face all impediments. Jupiter's aspect over the 3rd house makes him philosophical and learned as Jupiter also aspects the fifth house; the 6th lord is placed in the 7th house aspected by Jupiter. It makes the third the energetic and this energy is directed towards his service. He is, at present, the Managing Director of a bank. In *navamsa* the third house's lord is placed in the 6th house. As the planet is Moon, it indicates ups and downs in his service which is evident from the fact that on the grounds of false allegations he was suspended twice. But being learned and possessing requisite courage, he not only saved his service but also managed his promotions. He is a man of the devoted soul. It is evident from the fact that Jupiter and Sun aspect over the 3rd house, the house of tendency which clearly indicates pious, fighter of injustice, learned and a man of good qualities. He is successful in his service because he utilized his energy towards one goal, i.e. his service. Such qualities are attributed due to the aspect of Sun, Mercury and Jupiter over the 3rd house.

Example 5:

Born on 01.12.1965 at 1.30 p.m. at Agra

Balance of Rahu *mahadasa* at birth - 2Y 8M 12D

The 3rd house's lord is placed in the 11th house. Venus the lord of the 3rd house though placed in friendly sign, yet it has curtailed the capacity to work to a greater extent. Because

Birth Chart **Navamsa**

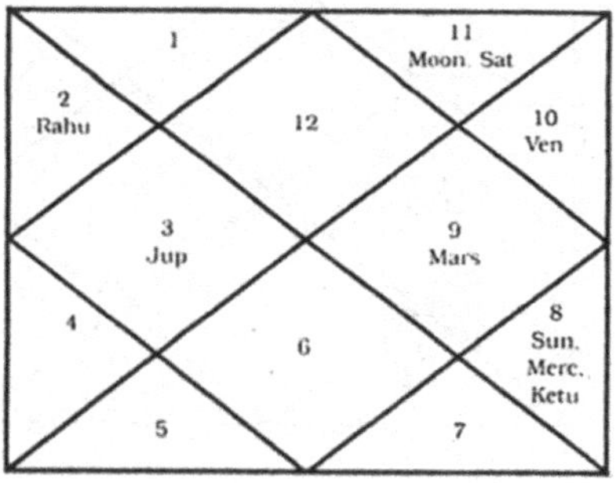

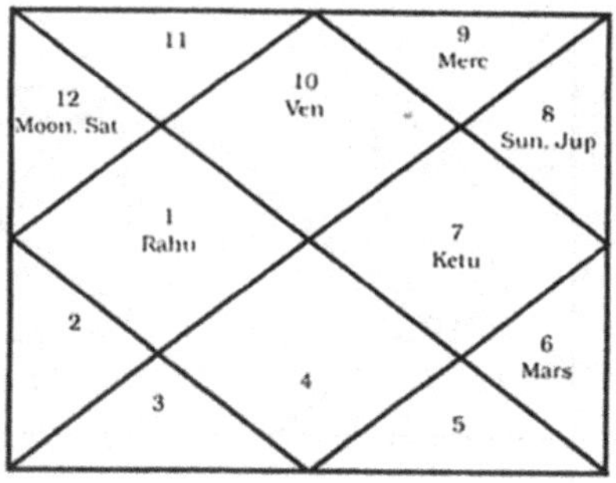

Venus, the planet of luxury and comfort, creates a pseudo feeling in native about his capacity because the 3rd house is the house of labour whereas its lord is significator of luxury. Contradictions are evident. Though the native is intelligent, learned yet with fickle mind. The lord of the 6th house is in formation of *Budh-Aditya Yoga*, however, the fickleness as contributed by Venus could not prepare him for any job. He is still jobless. Moon-Saturn conjunction though makes him plodding but has also generated fickleness. It is the aspect of Jupiter over the 3rd house that he is resorted to some meagre income. The lord of the 6th house in *navamsa* is aspected by Mars which has become afflicting. It also causes fickleness in him. Though man is learned, good-natured, intelligent yet he could not do anything in his life because to do any thing in life concentration is required which he lacks.

Example 6:

Born on 4.20 p.m. at 2.8.1966 at Agra.

Birth Chart **Navamsa**

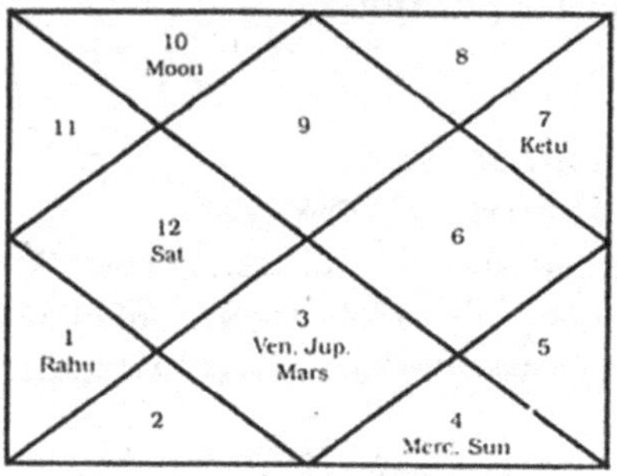

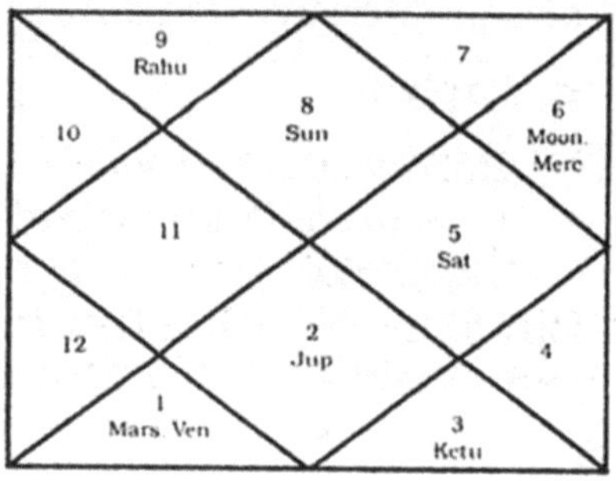

Balance of Jupiter Mahadasa at birth = 8Y 10M 16D

Birth star Punarvasu II pada

This chart belongs to a fierce and energetic young lady. She is at present councillor of *Nagar Nigam* of Agra. The third house is aspected by Jupiter alone. Her mental characteristics are primarily influenced by the lord of the 3rd house i.e. Saturn and Jupiter. Jupiter's aspect over the 3rd house has made her emotionally attached to her family, specially her younger brothers and sisters, whereas Saturn has made her more materialistic because the 4th house stands for materialism and placement of malefic like Saturn in the 4th house is not at all desirable and the problem is further aggravated if such Saturn is not aspected by any benefic planets. Sometimes, she behaves as if she is ardent follower of Charvak sect. As she is in active politics therefore only in this case the 10th house is to be analysed. The 10th lord is placed in the 8th house along with Sun causing *Budh-Aditya Yoga*. And this combination is aspected by the Moon. *Budh Aditya Yoga* in the 8th house is good because the 8th house happens to be the 11th house to the 10th house. But Moon's aspect over the 8th house is not desirable because such combination makes her to lose her control over mind and she is prone to burst out on a slight provocation. Further *Budh-Aditiya Yoga* makes the native learned but in this case, due to the aspect of Moon over the 8th house she has become quite practical. If she has to stay in politics she has to control her whims.

THE STUDY OF KRISHNAMURTY PADHATI IN RIGHT PERSPECTIVE

The great genius of astrology has been critised only for not following traditional astrology. If any astrologer without preconceived notion looks into the 'Six Readers' of Krishnamurty then it can be found out that he had first of all mentioned the rules of traditional astrology churned out from various literatures on astrology. His system of prediction may not be seen as discard of traditional astrology but be viewed as sincere efforts putting astrology on strong foot. Even though his own theory is rooted deep in traditional astrology. Sometimes, he had also used the principles of traditional astrology. I cite a few examples taken from his famous work 'Third Reader' which exhaustively deals with natal astrology. He had written on page 52 under the title 'Finance by borrowing', "Lord of the 12th house and Saturn generally cause loss by theft, fraud, deception, etc. and also due to the action of the secret enemies. People having Saturn in the 12th and Mars and Ketu in 2nd house, should be very careful. When they run the conjoined period of Saturn in the 12th and Mars and Ketu in the the 2nd house, or in the sub period of 6, 8 and 12, they will be taken to task. Even if Saturn is in the 3rd, 6th, or 10th house, brings about the sudden fall to the person."

All the ancient astrological texts as well as modern research scholars of astrology has verified this fact that Saturn in the 10th house gives spectacular rise in life but causes sudden fall to one's position. Nobody has offered any explanation about this sceptic behaviour of Saturn. Late Krishnamurty had explained this and reasoned the sudden fall of the native's position is due to the aspect of Saturn on the 12th house. It is a famous dictum of classical astrology that Saturn is the saviour of the *bhava* where it is posited, but lethal to those houses which are under its aspect. Here, rise of the native is linked up with the placement of Saturn either in the 3rd, 6th or 10th house, while fall is due to its aspect over the 12th house.

Another example which is cited on page 58 in the same

book reads as follows:

"You select either a Tuesday or a Saturday or a Sunday. On that day the *tithi* should be either *chaturtha*. Select Saturday and let the ascendant be in movable sign either Aries, Cancer, Libra or Capricorn."

In that example, he himself advocated absolute traditional astrology and cited the importance of *Hora* and *Tithi*. It is not out of place to mention here that he had written in the same book (from the page 329 to 347) about the magnificent importance of *Hora*. The importance of which in electional astrology is beyond doubt and accepted by all and sundry.

The entire astrological work gets its genesis into 'Brihat Parasara Hora Shashtra (BPHS)' which is said to deliver final verdict on any astrological rules. The rules of 'Nadh Shastra' are different from that of BPHS. I have personally encountered this problem while commenting over my recent book 'Sukh Nadi'. The principles laid down by sage Suka are different from that of either BPHS or 'Sarawali' or 'Brihat Samhita'. It does not mean that principles enunciated in 'Suka Nadi' are irrelevant or unvalid. They are valid provided in which conditions they will operate if known by astrologers. In the same way Krishnamurty made sincere and successful efforts to blend shattered principles into one knot and ultimately gave out one system as per his own logical and mental calibre.

In February 2001 issue of 'Times of Astrology' Mr. Rajendra Kumar has written very good article on Krishnamurty. I personally appreciate him for his knowledge, but also request him that K.P. system be put up in this way so that it could become a part of the daily life of all the astrologers. In other words, the complexity of this system be simplified so that it could be easily understood by all the astrologers. He has mentioned about 'Raz' theory which is said to be a later development. This theory does not seem to be as easy as its rules seem to be. The major problem is not the application of this theory but to prepare grounds for its applications. The role of astrologers who are following K.P. system is to set free this great work from its complexities and prepare simple rules which could be accepted by all and sundry. The theories, i.e. 'Gulbarga' theory, 'Paras fortuna' and new 'Raz' theory did not find place in 'Six Readers' of Krishnamurty as far as I remember. The above two theories viz. 'Gulbarga' theory and 'Paras fortuna' could not be find correct in its applications. I cannot comment on 'Raz' theory. Similarly, the ruling planets, actually told, were five in number but in later part the number increased subsequently from six to seven. In this way it shows our expertise on K.P. system but actually fails to deliver the motto of Late Krishnamurty.

The Krishnamurty system reaches its saturation point only when there is unique blending of rules of K.P. with that of the traditional astrology. The fundamental principles of traditional astrology beautifully be incorporated into K.P. system so that it could become a compendium of astrology. I have mentioned a few princeples of astrology in one of my articles published in the 'Times of Astrology' which were verified by me had been found to be correct and termed as fundamental principles of astrology. Such principles be churned out and applied to K.P. system. As mentioned somewhere in the article about 'Gulbarga' theory. This theory states if the sub lord of horary number or ascendant, as the case may be, happens to be either the Moon star lord or the *Lagna* star lord among the ruling planets, the desire of the native is fulfilled. This theory was substituted as follows:

"If Jupiter aspects ascendants in horary astrology at the time of judgement, desire of the native is fulfilled."

This principle was further magnified and reads as follows:

"If Jupiter aspects the concerned *bhava* related with query even then the desire of the native gets fulfilled." It was the finding which actually derived out while working on K.P. system.

The aim of citing this example is to make astrologers feel that K.P. system can be blended with traditional astrology too and this unique work of Krishnamurty must not fall victim to irrational criticism of the traditional astrologers.

I mention further few things in relation to example cited above:

The aspect of divine Jupiter either over ascendant or concerned *bhava* related with query must be strengthful, i.e. there should not be the sign of fall of Jupiter. If Capricorn sign happens to be either ascendant or concerned *bhava* then desire, if fulfilled, gets much delayed.

This observation further explains the reason why Krishnamurty considered *bhava* rather than sign. The debilitation of exaltation of planet actually reveals the strength of the planet rather than making it benefic or malefic. Our great seers advocated that exalted planet bestowing favourable results simply meant the planet in strength gives auspicious results.

What I personally felt is that the terminology used by Krishnamurty and later on by his followers also invited by a section of astrologers. Words like significators, ruling plantes, occupant, tenant, cusps, 'Gulbarg' theory, 'Raz' theory, etc. are few examples. These words be suitably with normal terminology as *bhava, swami*, etc.

It is not out of place to mention that 'Six Readers' of Krishnamurty is not an end but every open minded and research oriented scholar must take it as a beginning because each and every word mentioned in this book contains hidden treasure of game plan of planets. It depends on the astrologer himself or herself how beautifully he or she exploits it to the maximum benefit of human beings as well as to the service of astrology.

KRISHNAMURTY PADHATI - USEFUL GUIDELINES

In my previous article on 'Krishnamurty Padhati', I stressed upon the need of simplifying the procedure and also advocated the need of incorporating the fundamental principles of traditional astrology into it. The present article endeavours to further simplify the method enumerated by the great savant of astrology—Late K. S. Krishnamurty.

Role of the Moon and Ascendant

Moon is the significator of mind, therefore, tells about the mental state of the native. It clearly indicated the horary question asked by the querist is correct or the question put to test the knowledge of an astrologer. Our Upanishad says that the origin of words takes place at the level of soul and mind simply gets the reflection of this world. In this way there is mingling of mind with that of absolute nature of the word. Therefore, the true nature of desire never unfolds before an astrologer. The querist itself is unknown to this truth. In order to verify the actual desire of the native the sub lord of ascendant helps a lot. It has been found by us, in a number of cases, that in order to get a refined desire of the native sub lord of the ascendant has helped in every possible way. Therefore, it is imperative to look at the sub lord of the ascendant and then take up Moon. Whenever there is slight variation in the question asked by the querist or actual desire in the mind of the native the ascendant falls into the sub of Ketu or if sub lord of the ascendant does not show the matter with which query is related the native himself is found to be confused.

Affirmation or Negation of the Query

Late Krishnamurty had given one thumb rule to declare the query to be affirmative or negative. The thumb rules as per K.P. reads as follows:

If the sub lord of the eleventh cusp happens to be significator of the respective house, the query is to be answered in affirmation. There are other indications apart from this thumb rule which are enumerated below in concise and lucid manner.

Affirmation of Query

1. If Jupiter aspects ascendant in strength, the desire of the native gets fulfilled.

2. If Jupiter aspects concerned *bhava* which is related with query, even then desire gets fulfilled.

3. The sub lord of concerned *bhava* if posited in the 5th house, even then desire gets fulfilled. The reason is that from the 5th house sub lord aspects the 11th house which is the house of fulfilment of desires. The connection of the 5th and 11th houses is very vital clue in pronouncing the result to be affirmative in nature.

Negation of Query

1. If Jupiter does not aspect ascendant as well as concerned *bhava*.

2. If ruling planets are not related with significators of the houses related with query.

3. If any one of the ruling planets is retrograde.

4. If Rahu is posited in ascendant.

Comment: Late Krishnamurty has said that the retrograde planet neither loses energy nor strength. They are incapable of giving out results till they are retrograde. He has said again that the planet in retrogression if deposited in the constellation whose lord is in direct motion will give results when it becomes direct. I have found in a number of cases that if any planet in retrogression finds place among the ruling planets desire never gets fulfilled.

5. If the lord of ascendant is found to be debilitated.

6. If the sub lord of the eleventh cusp, though the significator of concerned houses, is found to be posited in houses like the 6th, 8th or 12th (if query not related with either borrowing or repayment of loans).

Comments: Serial numbers (1) and (2) both hold good in K.P. horary as well as in traditional horary astrology.

Aspects of Planets

Though late Krishnamurty explained a lot of things about the aspect of planets in his 'First Reader', yet he actually never made its use in practical cases dealt by him in Reader 3rd and 4th. He, however, made the use of aspects of a planet in an ordinary way as propounded in the traditional astrology. It seems to me that he was himself sceptic about the enlargement of scope of aspects on the western model. It is however my personal opinion that the western model on aspect is very scientific and actually forms the part of astronomy. Its major utility lies in both natal as well as horary astrology on the same analogy of importance of cuspal chart in prediction. I am not going in details of aspect as enumerated in various books on western astrology. What I simply propose to mention is that any adverse aspect between planet to planet or planet to house be given due weightage to know the pros and cons of the event.

It has been found by us that in horary astrology all the indicators responsible for the fructification of events failed to rectify the event in respect of time. Because at the time of judgement the aspect between planet to planet or planet to *bhava* concerned with query were not in favourable agreement. The event got materialized only when these planets where in favourable aspect with the concerned *bhava*.

Case Study

Purchase of land—when?
Horary no.-127
DOB : 01-02-2001
TOB : 10.07 a.m.
POB : Agra

This question was put by a lady and wanted to confirm whether her desire would be fulfilled or not, if fulfilled then when?

Step I

Cusps of houses	**Lord**	**Star lord**	**Sub lord**
1st cusp=6s-2d-40'	Venus	Mars	Venus
2nd cusp= 7s-1d-57'	Mars	Jupiter	Rahu
3rd cusp= 8s1d-57'	Jupiter	Ketu	Venus
4th cusp= 9s-3d-57'	Saturn	Sun	Saturn
5th cusp=10s-5d-57'	Saturn	Mars	Moon
6th cusp-11s-5d-57'	Jupiter	Saturn	Mercury

7th cusp=0s-2d-40'	Mars	Ketu	Venus
8th cusp=1s-2d-57'	Venus	Sun	Jupiter
9th cusp=2s-1d-57'	Mercury	Mars	Ketu
10th cusp=3s-3d-57'	Moon	Saturn	Saturn
11th cusp= 4s-5d-57'	Sun	Ketu	Rahu
12th cusp=5s-5d-57'	Mercury	Saturn	Mercury

Step II

Planetary Position	**Lord**	**Star lord**	**Sub lord**
Sun = 9s-18d-31'-29"	Saturn	Moon	Mercury
Moon = 0s-13d-47'-51"	Mars	Venus	Venus
Mars = 6s-28d-48'-50"	Venus	Jupiter	Sun
Merc = 10s-6d-5'-09"	Saturn	Mars	Moon
Jup = 1s-07d-24'-27"	Venus	Sun	Ketu
Ven = 11s-4d-43'-57"	Jupiter	Saturn	Saturn
Sat = 1s-0d-14'-53"	Venus	Sun	Rahu
Rahu = 2s-21d-18'-0"	Mercury	Jupiter	Jupiter
Ketu = 8s-21d-18'-0"	Jupiter	Venus	Jupiter

Confirmation of Desire

As mentioned above that desire is not only to be confirmed from the position of Moon but sub lord of ascendant should also be in the conformity of desire. If the sub lord of ascendant says something and the position of Moon presents another picture then desire is actually a hoax.

In this case study the Moon occupies Aries sign which is ruled by Mars, the natural significator of land. The sub lord of ascendant happens to be Venus and occupies the constellation of Saturn which rules the 4th house the natural house of landed properties. Thus the true nature of desire gets confirmed.

Affirmation or Negation of Desire

Purchase of land is denoted by the 2nd, 4th and 12th house. The 2nd house stands for liquid cash, while the 12th house denotes expenditure and the 4th house denotes land properties, i.e. liquid asset is converted into land by means of expenditure.

In this case Jupiter aspects the 12th house, the 2nd house and the 4th house. Therefore, confirmation of event is clearly visible. The aspect of Jupiter on the 4th house is debilitate, i.e. weak aspect as well as the sign Capricorn falls in the 4th house ruled by delaying the planet Saturn. Saturn too aspects the 4th house and considered *Rajyogakaraka* for Libra ascendant. Therefore, it may be inferred that after a delay and frustration the native is promised to get her desire fulfilled.

Aspects

As I have written somewhere in the article that all indications showing favourable results get miserably failed to rectify the event in want of proper aspect between planet and planet or planet and house concerned. Houses 2nd, 4th, 12th are related with the purchase of land and Jupiter is said to be the main instrument in fulfilling the desire of the native. Let us see what aspect Jupiter forms with these houses:

1. Jupiter is exact 143d-19' away from the 12th house and forming Biquintile aspect (Biquintile aspect 141-144d), since Jupiter is in direct motion and may be assumed moving forward—towards exact aspect. The Biquintile aspect is considered to be an auspicious aspect.
2. Jupiter is 157d-24d away from the 2nd house. This aspect falls between quincunx (148d-150d) and opposition (172d-180d), both these aspects are of adverse nature. Therefore, this aspect may be considered as adverse aspect.
3. Jupiter in 93d-24d away from the 4th house and forms square aspect. This aspect is also evil in nature.

Thus, the aspect Jupiter forms with these houses is more adverse in nature. It can be said that though Jupiter making good aspect with the 12th house ensures expenditure yet adverse aspects with the 2nd and 4th houses indicate delay in purchasing and even the purchased land may not yield good results to the native.

Similarly, the aspect of planets with planets may also be worked out and on the basis of good or evil nature of aspect conclusion may be drawn.

Comment: Since Jupiter is the significator of money and the fourth house indicates property. Aspect of Jupiter with the house ensures success. If one wants to make money through property transaction or wants to have significant results from one's own property then Mercury should form good aspect with Jupiter. Mercury governs business and Jupiter rules over money, therefore, business gives money only when Mercury is in good aspect with Jupiter. In this case study Mercury is 87d-19'away from Jupiter and forms square with Jupiter. This aspect is adverse in nature, therefore, the purchased land is not going to give any profit to the native at random. However, in transit, Mercury forms good aspect with Jupiter the property will yield good results.

Astrologer's Judgement

Though the native is destined to purchase land yet other factors indicate adverse results. The adverse result indicates that the native must be very careful while purchasing land. The delay is actually a bliss in disguise which gives time to time aspects of dealings.

Rectification of Event

Ruling planets

Asd lord = Venus
Asd star lord = Mars
Moon sign lord = Mars
Moon star lord = Venus
Day ruled by = Jupiter

Venus *mahadasa* and Venus *antardasa* extend upto 22 Sept 2003.

Venus *mahadasa*, Venus *antardasa* and Mars *sookshma* operate form 23 May 2001 to 2 Aug 2001.

Thus, during the period form 23rd May 2001 to 2nd Aug 2001 land is likely to be purchased.

The agreement of purchasing was signed on 31st May 2001 and a handsome amount was paid to the seller.

The final registry of the purchased land is to be made on 15th August. However, in my opinion the actual registry will be made after 29th August 2001 when Venus/Venus/Rahu/Jupiter period would be operating because Jupiter is one of the ruling planets.

THE IMPORTANCE OF SUB LORD IN DECIDING EDUCATIONAL DISCIPLINE

Education itself manifests broad concept of learning of all subjects though its utility lies in achieving a particular goal. However, its scope has been reduced to a few items of learning relegating its background, its broad meaning and aim. Today, education becomes important due to two superficial concepts of society, i.e. social status and secondly a passport to job. The real and valuable aim of education, i.e. to make man a good citizen and saviour of society, has lost completely. The prime object of education, in present context, is to secure a proper job too has failed due to want of particular skill or expertise in a particular job. Today, in world, keeping in view the requirements of various jobs, new education policies introducing new subjects have gained upper hands which were not known even ten years back. Therefore, to assign these subjects to a particular planet has become a daunting task to astrologers. The ancient classical astrological texts have assigned following subjects to following planets:

1. Sun : Medicine
2. Moon : Study concerned with sea, river, etc.
3. Jupiter : Study of Vedas and holy scriptures.
4. Venus : Chemistry, beauty
5. Mars : Engineering
6. Mercury : Commerce
7. Saturn : Philosophy, occultism, *mantra-tantra*, etc.

With the advent of new economic policies on the world horizon various new subjects have popped up to meet the requirements and requisite standard of these services. In the light of these statements following subjects have been assigned to particular planets.

1. Sun	:	Medicine
2. Moon	:	Commerce, agriculture, meteorological vedic knowledge, astrology, etc.
3. Jupiter	:	Banking, journalism, etc.
4. Venus	:	Chemistry, agriculture, biology, vocal music or instrumental music.
5. Mars	:	Engineering, accountancy, mathematics.
6. Mercury	:	Journalism, banking, astrology, scientific researches, etc.
7. Saturn	:	Philosophy, occult sciences, mining, mountaineering, forestry, computer education etc.

The houses in astrology which deal with education chiefly are 4th and 5th. The 4th house stands for mundane and practical education which is required in day to day activities in life, while the 5th house deals with the divine knowledge such as *vedas*, astrology, *mantra-tantra*, etc. It is also imperative to look into the 3rd house because this house shows the tendencies of the native tendencies and plays vital role in selecting the subjects of studies well suited to the native according to his or her temperament and general tendencies, i.e. liking or disliking for the subjects.

It is also important to mention here that for a good academic life one should have strong 5th house.

Before taking up actual live cases for studies it's important that as far as education is concerned one must take into account the sub lord of the 4th and 5th cusp and *Niryan Bhava Chalit Kundali*, the importance of which is continuously stressed upon by the learned editor of this magazine. It is also important to mention here that graduation or post graduation in any discipline may or may not fetch a job.

Example 1: DOB : 20.5.1974
TOB : 11.24 p.m.
POB : Agra

The sub lord of the 4th cusp is Saturn which is placed in 5th house while the sub lord of the 5th cusp is placed in the 5th house. The 4th house is occupied by the Moon while in Krishnamurty chart the 4th house is occupied by the Sun and the 5th house is occupied by Saturn, Mercury and Ketu.

The native is well qualified and has seen a lot of fluctuations in his academic life.

(i) The native got his graduation with biology and chemistry.

(ii) He later on completed MBA and computer diploma.

(iii) He got his post graduation in economics.

The native was a science graduate but completely switched over to professional qualifications like MBA and economics.

In birth chart the conjugation of Sun-Mercury in the sign of Venus in the 5th house gave him science education with chemistry as one of the subjects up to graduation. In *Niryana* cuspal chart the Sun shifted back to the 4th house clearly indicates that the association of the native with science subjects will be for a long time due to segregation of the Sun with Mercury. The sub lords of the 4th cusp and 5th cusp are placed in the 5th house. Therefore, the native always came out with flying colours as far as his education is concerned. Mercury, the planet of accounts, gave him the education of MBA and economics. Saturn provided him with computer knowledge. Now let us look at the 3rd house, the 3rd house is occupied by the exalted Venus and in *Niryana Bhava Chalit* Moon too is posited there in. Moon-Venus association makes one imaginative but unstable in one's approach. The exalted Venus made him fond of easy money and lavish life style. Thus, the basic tendency of this native did not allow him to set up any clear cut goal in his life. The 4th lord is placed in the 6th house. The 6th house happens to be the 3rd house to the 4th house it again shows basic tendencies and inclination in respect of his education. Here the lord is Mars which is natural malefic and makes the native rash and unprudent in deciding his career in respect of his education.

Whenever the lord of the 4th house or significator of knowledge like Mercury and Jupiter is placed in the 6th and 8th houses the native, though highly qualified, can not utilize his education for the general purpose it is meant for. Contrary to this, the native becomes well versed in various subjects and he may easily be adorned with the title—jack of all trades.

Example 2: DOB: 16.11.1966
TOB: 8.17 p.m.
POB: Delhi

The sub lord of the 4th cusp is Rahu which is placed in the 11th house. The sub lord of the 5th cusp is Venus which is placed in the 6th house in the birth chart and shifts back to the 5th house in *Niryana* cuspal chart. The lord of the 4th house is Mercury which is placed in the 6th house in the birth chart, while shifts back to the 5th house in cuspal chart. The lord of the 5th house is Venus which too is placed in the 6th house, while shifts back to the 5th house in cuspal chart. The sub lord of the 4th cusp is Rahu which is natural malefic and whenever gets connected with the 4th house brings down the quality of that house. But thanks to the Almighty that the lord of the 4th and 5th houses and the sub lord of the 5th house are natural benefic. The native did B.Sc. with physics, chemistry and maths and later on did law. Mercury-Sun conjunction with Venus gave him science knowledge with chemistry as one of the subjects. The lord of the 5th and 4th houses are aspected by Mars-Saturn making them weak to give the results which they ought to give. Mars-Saturn and Rahu influenced his planets of education and turned him to study law—Saturn-Rahu influenced. Mars-Saturn when jointly or individually influencing the native then once in his life time the native comes into the contact of judiciary or related field where the authority has power to prosecute the person.

In this case Mars is the lord of the 11th house while Saturn is the lord of the ninth house. Therefore, two malefics indicate his way of income generation. Rahu makes one secretive in one's activities. The sub lord of the 4th cusp, i.e. the house of practical knowledge is influenced by Rahu and Mercury. Mercury is in conjunction with the Sun forming *Budh-Aditya Yoga*. The *yoga* itself makes the native intelligent. The secretive intelligence is used for the profession of law.

Example 3: DOB : 10.11.1934
TOB : 8.28 p.m.
POB : Allahabad

The lords of the 4th and 5th houses are Mercury and Venus respectively which are placed in the 5th house along with Jupiter and Sun. The placement of three benefics in the 5th house causes *Saraswati Yoga*. The attribute of this *yoga* is that native is learned, gentle, intelligent, well versed in various subjects. The sub lord of the 4th cusp is Jupiter which is placed in the 5th house. The sub lord of the 5th cusp is Moon which is placed in the 7th house but shifts back to the 6th house in cuspal chart. The native is lawyer, poet, astrologer and well versed in various subjects. The blending of many traits in one personality is due to *Saraswati Yoga*.

The native was never restricted to the study of any particular subject. However up to graduation the native was the student of arts subject viz. Hindi, English, History, etc.

Later on, he got law degree and became a lawyer. He switches over to law discipline in all probability is related with his forthcoming profession due to the influence of stars. Saturn aspects the 10th house, and Mars too aspects the 10th house. Thus, his 10th house i.e. the lord of the 6th and 11th houses, the house of profession was influenced by two worst malefics. Due to this influence the native may be criminal but three benefics aspects the 11th house. Therefore, the native won disputes or persons which were involved in litigations. Since the sub lords of the 4th and 5th houses are benefic like Jupiter and Mars, therefore, native shows his inclination in various subjects.

Example 4: DOB : 24.4.1973
TOB : 8.45 a.m.
POB : Bhind Morena

The lords of the 4th and 5th houses are the Sun and Mercury respectively. The sub lord of the 4th cusp is Venus while the sub lord of the 5th cusp is Saturn. In birth chart the Sun and Venus are placed together in the 12th house, while in cuspal chart both the planets shift to the 12th house. Venus and Sun as lords of the 4th and 5th houses respectively aspect the 5th house. Two planets related with service and education made the native to study science subjects up to graduation. He did B.Sc. and later got M.A. in history. The sub lord of the 5th cusp is Saturn which is known as the planet with seperative tendencies is placed in ascendant in friendly sign but shifts back to the 12th house in cuspal chart. Since the sub lord of the 5th cusp, i.e. Saturn itself is the planet of separative and unsteady nature is placed in the 12th house, the malefic one. This planetary disposition clearly indicates that the native did not have any proper aim while deciding his academic career. He completed has M.A in history due to the influence of Mercury and Jupiter. In birth chart Mercury and Jupiter aspect the 5th house while in cuspal chart both the planets aspect the 4th house. Mars too aspects the 4th house. Thus, both the houses of education come under the influence of Mercury, Jupiter, Mars, Sun and Venus. These are Mercury and Jupiter which were mainly responsible to his switch over to post graduation in history. However, his income source is related with science subjects specially with the Sun. The native is a medical representative— the career which is strongly denoted by the Sun because of its placements in the 11th house. The aspect of the other planets on the 4th house could make him financially viable.

Example 5: DOB : 21.07.1972
TOB : 9.05 p.m.
POB : Morena

The lord of the 4th and 5th houses are Venus and Mercury respectively. The sub lord of the 4th and 5th cusp are Ketu and Mercury. She is throughout arts student, i.e. she did B.A., M.A. and Ph.D in geography. In cuspal chart the sub lord of the 4th cusp is placed in the 5th house. Ketu, Rahu Saturn are the planets which are related with subject like geography. Ketu is placed in the 5th house and Saturn is placed in the 4th house. Though Venus is placed in the 4th house and the Sun is placed in the 5th house must invariably give scientific education. Since Sun is placed in the sixth house being the lord of the seventh house and neither it is the sub lord of the 4th nor 5th cusp. Venus too is not the sub lord of either the 4th or 5th cusp. The primary education factor is determined by the sub lords. In this cusp Ketu being the sub lord of the 4th cusp is placed in the 5th cusp extends influence over both the houses. This was the main reason that she got post graduation in a particular subject like geography.

Example 6: DOB : 1.04.1976
TOB : 8.05 p.m.
POB : Morena

The lord of the 4th and 5th houses are the Moon and the Sun respectively. The sub lords of the 4th and 5th cusps are Moon and Saturn respectively. Saturn is placed in the 4th house in the birth chart but shifts back to the 3rd house in cuspal chart. The sub lord of the 4th cusp Moon is placed in ascendant but goes to the 12th house in cuspal chart. The native is post graduate in science. She did M.Sc. in chemistry. In cuspal chart the 4th house is aspected by Jupiter while in the birth chart Jupiter aspects the 5th house. In both the cases the aspect of Jupiter over both the houses promise good and complete education. The aspect of Venus over the 5th house and in cuspal chart the aspect of Mars and Saturn over the 5th house gave him science education with Venus as one of the principal subject. In a number of cases it has been seen when Mars, Venus, Sun and Saturn individually or collectively influence the 5th house, the native reads about chemicals. Since the lords of the 4th and 5th houses go to the 12th house in cuspal chart, therefore, native is not likely to get benefit of her qualification.

The bookish or college education simply makes one eligible to be called as a literate. It is only his or her strong knowledge of various subjects which win him or her the title 'educated'.

DISCUSSION ON THE EFFICACY OF KRISHNAMURTY PADHATI

(Rectification of Birth Time)

There are various methods to find out birth details of the native. 'Nastajatkam' translated by Late R. Santhanam deals with the subject exhaustively. Similarly, other texts also deal with the subject completely or partially depending upon the own way of understanding the subject by the scholars of astrology. K. P. system in dealing with the subject also presents a system of its own utility and much depends on the calibre of the native how beautifully he or she picks up the contents of the subject.

How to Find Out the Time of Birth Using K.P. System

One of the governors of Indian states has his date of birth but does not have time of birth; even he did not remember whether he was born during daytime or night. Even *Krishnamurti Padhati* too dealing with such questions requires at least approximate birth time, i.e. whether native is born during day or night. In that particular case the native gave only D.O.B. but could not mention the approximate time of birth. He was asked to mention one number between 1 to 249.

He mentioned number 99.

1. In majority of cases it has been found that the number mentioned by the querist shows one's ascendant if one has real urge.
2. The chosen number also denotes one's personality, behaviour, profession, etc., i.e. ascendant as per number shows basic foundation of the native on which rests one's future events.

The number 99 as mentioned by Honourable Governor shows Leo sign ruled by the Sun. Since the Sun is the natural significator of Constitution, Judges, Governors and President of India. In case of other political dignitaries who are elected through the votes of public, the rising sign may be different but whenever we talk about the persons who are acting on behalf of the Constitution of India, are always predominantly ruled by the Sun.

The Honourable Governor gave that number which showed his present portfolio and also his birth ascendant as Krishnamurty said that if during an interaction over horary astrology somebody put up his birth chart, the ruling planets of the birth chart and ruling planets at the time of judgement of any query are always the same.

The query was taken up for judgement on 21.07.2000 at 8.20 p.m.

1. The ascendant was in Leo sign ruled by the Sun, star lord Venus and sub lord Ketu.
2. Ruling Planets
    - (i) Asd lord = Sun
    - (ii) Asd star lord = Venus
    - (iii) Moon sign lord = Jupiter
    - (iv) Moon star lord = Jupiter
    - (v) Day ruled by = Venus (Friday)
3. The birth details of the native must agree with the ruling planets as strongly propounded by Late Krisnamurty.
4. On that basis I selected the time of birth 4.27 a.m.
5. The sub lord Ketu of horary no. 99 could not find place among the ruling planets.
6. The esteemed reader will be surprised to note that on dated 1.10.1928 at 4.27 a.m., the moon was passing through 'Aswini Star' ruled by Ketu. Therefore, all the ruling planets become in agreement with the lord, star lord or sub lord of horary no. 99. Therefore, the birth details after these calculation were found to be DOB 1.10.1928, TOB 4.27 a.m. POB Ambala.

The ascendant was in 45 20d- 11' -28" ruled by the Sun, star, lord Venus and sub lord Jupiter.

Jupiter comes twice in the list of ruling planets. Similarly, Venus also comes twice among the list of ruing planets. It is also interesting that on dated 1.10.1928 at 4.27 a.m. *Navamsa* ascendant fell in Libra sign ruled by Venus.

DISCUSSION ON THE EFFICACY OF KRISHNAMURTY PADHATI

Human history itself is the witness of man's progress from the stone age to the nuclear age. The human beings with their roots in the barbaric society made onward march to the semi civilized society and made subsequent progress in all directions influencing all aspects of the human life. Principal requirements the of human life ultimately forced man to tread on the path of innovation and research. The main tool used to achieve progress was human mind. Similarly, to achieve progress in metaphysical world the another tool of human personality, i.e. intuition, is used. Though divine principles are, in general, beyond the approach of normal common sense and cannot be apprehended only from rational point of view. The perception of divine principles can only be made when native is endowed with some sort of divinity in awakened state. Therefore, astrology may be studied and practiced by only those persons who have some sort of divinity, in alive state, as present in them. Astrologers play with the stars and planets and become links between cosmos and earth.

Since astrology is the work of pure intuition, therefore, the absolute realism cannot effectively deal with the intricate principles of astrology handed over to us by the great seers like, Maharsi Parasara, Kalidas, Mantreshwara, etc. Astrologers are baffled and perplexed at the various principles of astrology given to us by these seers and find no logical explanations to this riddle. The answer of this riddle cannot be given with a rational approach because the question itself is beyond the reach of human mind. The simple answer to this riddle of various principles of astrology may be that astrology is the work of intuition and the great seers with their different intuition powers saw the different permutations and combinations of light emanating from different planets of the solar system and their effects upon human beings. Different sages with different intuitive capacities experienced the game of light in different ways. Therefore, these different principles at the first sight seem to be different from each other, but even then the some sort of uniformity is seen in all these different principles, i.e. (i) all the sages established the role of planets in shaping human destiny. In modern times two great astrologers appeared on the horizon of astrology, viz. Prof. Krishnamurty and Dr. B. V. Raman. Dr. B.V. Raman endeavoured very much to enrich the Indian astrology and was also instrumental in disseminating the real values of Vedic astrology out of India. With his knowledge and god-gifted intuition he not only translated ancient astrological work but also simplified very complicated principles of astrology. It is due to the sincere service of this man that very complicated principles of astrology became easily comprehensible for astrologers with common intellect. He not only spread the knowledge of astrology in South India but also in north India. The entire astrological folk is indebted to this great savant of astrology. The another genius of astrology, Late Prof. Krishnamurty, enriched the vedic astrology with modern thinking and sharp intellect. His entire work, demonstrates, his innovative thinking which could not be expected during the time he flourished because between 1960 to 1970 the average I.Q. was not much higher. During that time an astrologer breaking the old traditional system of prognostication dared to put a new method of reading future events and brought the concept of sub lord theory. This man was ridiculed and criticized for his new system of prognostication, not because it was in line with traditional system of astrology but of new idea he had given to the astrological world. Though the mention of '*Krishnamurty Padhati*' among astrologers irks them. Every new idea first brings suspicion and criticism because it seems to be a foreign concept to the indigenous way of thinking, but when this new idea becomes the necessity of time people accolades the giver. If one sincerely and truly looks back at the history of development of astrology then except '*Krishnamurty Padhati*' we have nothing new which really be called a research work forget that he had not invented any new planet and new constellation or he had not given a new *dasa* system. He simply delineated the scattered various principles of astrology mentioned in ancient works of astrology. Even today astrologers read only the ancient books but never try to read between the lines.

The entire world—its evolution or dissolution, the rotation and revolution of the earth, the motion of planets, and at last but not least the human journey from infant to old all are nothing but the super game of time. The efficacy of '*Krishnamurty Padhati*' lies in the fact that he was a pioneer in bringing the conception of time in astrology more predominantly. The '*Krishnamurty Padhati*' in subtle form is nothing but the division of time. The *vimshottari dasa* system, one hundred and twenty years old, covers twenty seven constellations of zodiac. Prof. Krishnamurty divided twenty seven constellations into 249 divisions. In this way he expanded the dimension of time covering those details of planets which are hidden from human perception and also helped to pinpoint the exact behaviour of planets.

Few Important Tips (Application of Krishnamurty)

1. '*Krishnamurty Pandhati*' actually revamped system of traditional horary astrology, chiefly deals with the horary system of astrology. It is imperative to clear here the question, why '*Krishnamurty Padhati*' deals with horary astrology? The answer is that human beings are always under the constant watch of the planets. The horary astrology reveals the effect of the planets on a particular moment. It also acts as a tool between the effects of the planets and the agitation of mind. Therefore, the system ropes into three important factors of the universe, i.e. time (the moment of question), mind (the tool of desire) and planets (the source of light). Therefore, it is said that the natal astrology has its own limitations but horary astrology never fails.

2. The above statement has been verified by me on several occasions. It has been experienced on several times that the query put by the querist from of any part of India even on telephone always coincide with the number as given by the querist. I was also a bit surprise to see the amazing results that the ascendant shown by number, was the same when ascendant as per traditional system was worked out.

3. The system is unique in foretelling the results of the query and one can say out rightly with confidence the answer in either affirmation or negation. The system also helps in timing the events. (Due to problems of *ayanamsa* timing of events have differed from fifteen days to one months but the result was always the same as predicted).

4. The system reveals more elaborately the role of Saturn and the retrograde planets. Since the behaviour of retrograde planet is still a mystery for the astrologers. Some astrologers say that planet in retrogression losses its strength, while some say that retrograde planet gives the result of previous house and so on. I am not in position to give my preference to any view but experience has shown me that retrogression is always linked up with negation. In majority of cases I have found that whenever query in any way is connected with retrograde planet it could not get materialized. It has also helped me to give my verdict in clear terms 'Yes' or 'No'.

Saturn is always found to be delayed planets. It not only gives delay but tortures and torments the native to such extent that one may think to commit suicide but also showers its benevolence on the native by fulfilling his desires. Therefore, the native having either Capricorn or Aquarius ascendants be ready to face humiliations and dejections with the hope that if *winter comes spring be far behind.* They are always successful in long run. The politicians with either Capricorn or Aquarius ascendant must not hope for early success. Success is endowed on them only in old age.

5. The aspect of Jupiter and Saturn are more pronounced then their placements. These two planets always bring big events of life due to their aspect. The placement of Jupiter either in ascendant, 5th and 9th houses always make the native happy. It has also been seen that the placement of Jupiter in after the 2nd aforesaid houses makes the native indifferent in his approach. The placement of Jupiter in ascendant brings him divine help and protection. The native is endowed with male issues and is religious. Jupiter in the 5th house makes the native to explore new avenues of income and he is assisted by his close relatives in his income generation. He is fond of reading and writing but he himself is neither eloquent writer nor good speaker. He gets recognition due to divine help. The Jupter in the 9th house makes one good writer and he always gets profits from publication or journalism. The aspect of Saturn always hampers the results of the concerned *bhava* to manifest. As I said above, the Saturn being ascendant lord or being *yogakaraka* planet fructifies the result after dejections and denials.

6. If the ascendant of horary horoscope is aspected by Jupiter, the desires of the querist are fulfilled. The positive

results further become pronounced, when apart ascendant, Jupiter aspects the concerned *bhava* too. If Saturn too aspects the concerned *bhave* then it is clear testimony that after a delay, desire is fulfilled.

7. It has also been observed severaltimes, that whenever Saturn predominantly influences any of the concerned *bhava* which is devoid of any benefic aspect the desire of the querist is not fulfilled. Similarly, if Saturn and Mars become lord and sub lord of the concerned *bhava*, the results are cruel in nature.

Let us discuss a few peculiar cases which in many instances can not be predicted accurately with the help of natal astrology.

Example 1: One person wanted to know the sex of the child yet to be born. As his wife was in the family way. He mentioned the no. 124.

The query was taken up instantly on the same day. The synopsis of the procedure adopted is as follows:

Day of judgement	Wednesday
Date of judgement	05.04.2000
Time of judgement	8.30 p.m.
Place of judgement	Agra

The cusp chart of the number 124 is as follows:

Cusp	**Sign lord**	**Star lord**	**Sub lord**
1st Cusp = 5S7d-53'	Mercury	Mars	Saturn
2nd Cusp = 6s 26d–48'	Venus	Jupiter	Venus
3rd Cusp = 7s 26d–48'	Mars	Mercury	Jupiter
4th Cusp = 8s 28d-48'	Jupiter	Sun	Mars
5th Cusp = 10s 0d-48'	Saturn	Mars	Mercury
6th Cusp = 11s 0d-48'	Jupiter	Jupiter	Mars
7th Cusp = 11s 27d-53'	Jupiter	Mercury	Jupiter
8th Cusp = 0s 26d-48'	Mars	Sun	Sun
9th Cusp = 1s 26d-48'	Venus	Mars	Jupiter
10th Cusp = 2s 28d-48'	Mercury	Jupiter	Sun
11th Cusp = 4s 0d-48'	Sun	Ketu	Venus
12th Cusp = 5s 0d-48'	Mercury	Sun	Rahu

Note: The cusps were worked out using Raphel's table of house division, and Krishnamurty *aynamsa*.

I predicted to be born child a female. The reason is that:

1. The ascendant itself was female sign.
2. The 5th cusp falls in female sign and the sub lord of the

5th cusp is Mercury, a feminine planet.

3. The sub lord of 11th cusp was Venus a feminine planet.

4. In cuspal chart Saturn is placed in the 7th house, aspecting ascendant. Saturn being a faminine planet.

5. The 5th house in cuspal chart was occupied by Mercury.

6. The ascendant and the houses concerned with the query were under the dominating influence of the female planet viz. Mercury, Saturn and Venus.

7. The 7th house was occupied by Sat, Mars and Jupiter. Though Saturn, Mars and Jupiter aspect ascendant, yet this only ensure that there would be no harm to the child to be born.

8. Jupiter is said to be *Putrakaraka*. In order to get at least must aspect the 10th house because the 10th house denotes final rituals of the father which in a hindu family are done by the son. In that case Jupiter did not aspect the 10th house. Therefore, the last hope of getting a male child was also lost.

Note: The anxious father next day rushed for an ultrasound of her wife and a bit surprise to esteemed readers that my prediction was one hundred per cent correct.

Example 2: The another example is also peculiar in nature in the sense that it is related with very interesting question: Do astrologers too attend the horoscope only when they are allowed by the stars? The answer is as follows:

1. In case of natal astrology one can make predications even while moving in the train, if the horoscope is put before him. The predications came out true or not it does not matter.

2. In case of answering horary question, it is the time selected by the stars itself. It is out of free will of the astrologer to select the time. How this happens let us see with the following examples:

One person mentioned no. 13 and wanted to know about his future prospects in his own department.

The query was taken up for judgement on dated 1st April 2000 at 7.24 p.m. at Agra. However, in the middle of the exercise, I was instantly required to attend an another personal business, therefore, I left the exercise to be resumed only at 8.34 p.m. on the same date and place.

Note: It was the first experience of its kind I had to put off exercise in middle otherwise without any single failure, I even completed exercise on horary in one stroke. Therefore, I was naturally forced to think over this brake down.

Analysis: The cusp for No. 13 using Krishnamurty *aynamsa*. Are as follows:

Cusp	**Sign lord**	**Star lord**	**Sub lord**
1st Cusp = 0s17d-20'	Mars	Venus	Mars
2nd Cusp = 1s16d-47'	Venus	Moon	Saturn
3rd Cusp = 2s10d-47'	Mercury	Rahu	Jupiter
4th Cusp = 3s 4d-47'	Moon	Saturn	Saturn
5th Cusp = 4s 2d-47'	Sun	Ketu	Venus
6th Cusp = 5s 6d-47'	Mercury	Sun	Mercury
7th Cusp = 6s17d-20'	Venus	Rahu	Venus
8th Cusp = 7s16d-47'	Mars	Mercury	Mercury
9th Cusp = 8s10d-47'	Jupiter	Ketu	Saturn
10th Cusp = 9s 4d-47'	Saturn	Sun	Saturn
11th Cusp = 10s 2d-47'	Saturn	Mars	Ketu
12th Cusp = 11s 6d-47'	Jupiter	Saturn	Mercury

2. Ruling planets at 7.24 p.m.
   Ascendant lord = Mars
   Ascendant star lord = Venus
   Moon sign lord = Saturn
   Moon star lord = Rahu
   Day ruled by Saturn

3. Ruling planets at 8.34 p.m.
   Ascendant lord = Mars
   Ascendant star lord = Venus
   Moon sign lord = Saturn
   Moon star lord = Rahu
   Day ruled by Saturn

It has been observed that ascendant is shown by querist while the seventh house is shown by the astrologer because the 7th house shows partnership and the interaction between the querist and the astrologer is some sort of partnership for specific purpose. Therefore, the sub lord of ascendant should be the significator of the 7th cusp or the sub lord of the 7th cusp must be significator of sub lord of ascendant.

At 7.24 p.m. the ascendant as per traditional method was 6s-29d-56' – 05" star lord Mars and sub lord Saturn. The sub lord Saturn of the rising ascendant was neither the significator of the 7th cusp nor it was related in any way with the 7th cusp. Therefore, the broke down relationship between the astrologer and querist took place.

At 8.34 p.m. the rising sign was Libra 6s15d-14' – 46" star lord Rahu and the sub lord Venus. The 7th cusp has sub lord Venus. Thus ascendant at 7.24 p.m. moved to that position of zodiac which was ruled by the planets signifying the 7th house. In this way relationship between the astrologer and querist was established. Therefore, it is advisable in all the cases whether it is natal astrology or horary the ascendant and the seventh house must bear any sort of relationship.

Discussion on the Efficacy of '*Krishnamurti Padhati*'

Example 3: One person wanted to know about the clearance of his loan from the bank. He personally appeared before me and gave the number 146.

The query was taken up for judgement on dated 06.06.2000 at 8.34 p.m. at Agra. The cusps for no. 146 using Krishnamurti *Aynamsa* are as follows:

Cusp	Sign lord	Star lord	Sub lord
1st Cusp = 7s 0°-0'	Mars	Jup	Moon
2nd Cusp =7s 29°-33'	Mars	Merc	Sat
3rd Cusp = 9s 1°-33'	Sat	Sun	Jup
4th Cusp =10s 5°-33'	Sat	Mars	Sun
5th Cusp = 11s 7°-33'	Jup	Sat	Ketu
6th Cusp = 0s 5°-33'	Mars	Ketu	Mars
7th Cusp = 1s 0°-0'	Ven	Sun	Rahu
8th Cusp = 1s 29°-33'	Ven	Mars	Sat
9th Cusp = 3s 1°-33'	Moon	Jup	Rahu
10th Cusp = 4s 5°-33'	Sun	Ketu	Mars
11th Cusp = 5s 7°-33'	Merc	Sun	Ketu
12th Cusp = 6s 5°-33'	Ven	Mars	Sun

Cuspal Chart

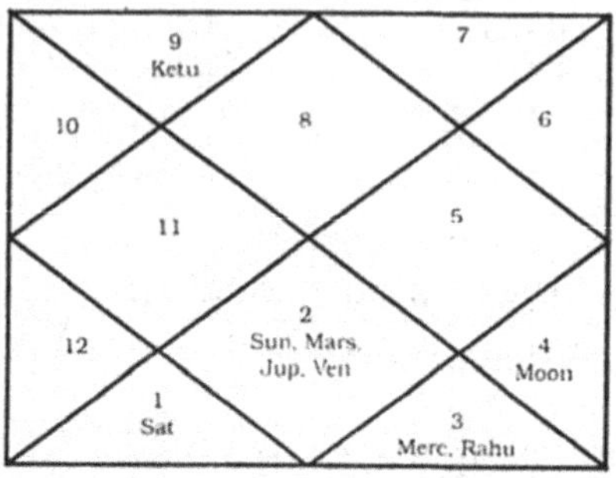

If one wants to borrow then the 6th house is judged. I have verified through my findings that whenever at the time of query Jupiter ascpects ascendant then the query is materialized.

In this case, Jupiter not only aspects ascendant but also the 11th house. Therefore, he is able to borrow from the bank. Since Mars happens to be sub lord of the 6th cusp and aspects ascendant. Therefore, there may be some problems in getting loan from bank. When will he receive the loan?

Ruling Planets

1- Asd Lord= Mars
2- Asd Star Lord= Jup
3- Moon Sign Lord= Moon
4- Moon Star Lord=MC
5- De Lord= MC

The *dasa* at the time of query was Mercury *mahadasa* and Venus *bhukti* which ended on 3 Nov 2001. Venus is in the star of Moon which happens to be the lord of the 9th house. *Mahadasa* coincides with the ruling planets. Therefore, during this period he may get loan from the bank.

Example 4: One person wanted to repay his loan, he gave number 151. The question was judged on dated 10.07.2000 at 9.11 a.m. at Agra.

The cusps for number 151 are as follows:

Cusp	Sign lord	Star lord	Sub lord
1st Cusp= 7s 7°-20'	Mars	Sat	Ketu
2nd Cusp=8s 6°-32'	Jup	Ketu	Rahu
3rd Cusp= 9s 10°-32'	Sat	Moon	Moon
4th Cusp=10s 14°-32'	Sat	Rahu	Ketu
5th Cusp= 11s 16°-32'	Jup	Sat	Jup
6th Cusp = 0s 13°-32'	Mars	Ven	Ven
7th Cusp= 1s 7°-20'	Ven	Sun	Ketu

Cuspal Chart

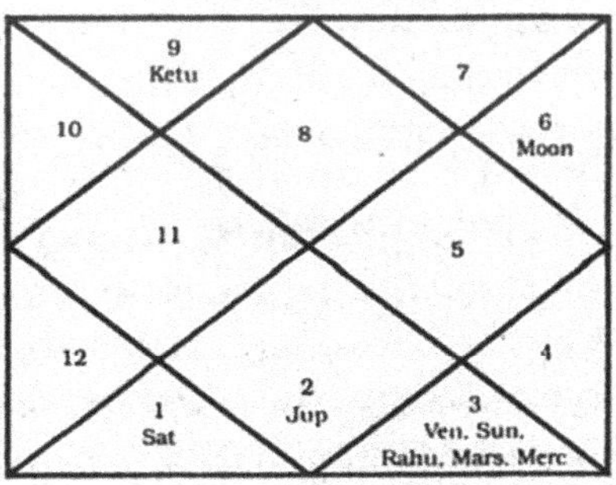

8th Cusp= 2S 6°-32'	Merc	Mars	Moon
9th Cusp=3S 10°-32'	Moon	Sat	Sun
10th Cusp= 4S 14°-32'	Sun	Ven	Ven
11th Cusp= 5S 16°-32'	Merc	Moon	Sat
12th Cusp= 6S 13°-32'	Ven	Rahu	Merc

In this case, also Jupiter aspects ascendant. Therefore, querist's desire is sure to be fulfilled. If the sub lord of 12th cusp is placed in the constellation of the planet whose lord is in retrograde motion then desire is not fulfilled. In the third case sub lord itself is retrograde and placed in the star of Rahu (As Rahu has always been in retrograde motion.) Therefore, Rahu is not considered as retrograde planet. Therefore, two contradictory results are obtained.

1. Jupiter aspect over ascendant ensures that querist will repay the loan.
2. The sub lord of the 12th cusp Mercury desires repayment of loan. The conclusion is that when Mercury 18° gets direct motion desire is fulfilled.

The *dasa* at the time of query was Rahu *mahadasa* and Mercury *antardasa* upto 17 Nov 2001.

There will be delay and later on the native would be able to clear his loan because Rahu first gives the results of the planets with which it is conjoined — Mercury, Venus, Mars, etc. Secondly, Rahu is in the star of Jupiter which happens to be *yogakarka*. Therefore, after some initial problems the native will start repayment of his loan in installments because Mercury itself shows repayment in installments.

Example 5: One person wanted to know about his case in the High Court, Delhi. He gave me number 201. The question was taken up for judgement on 06.06.2000 at 10.29 p.m. at Agra.

Note: For this particular question, 2 did not workout cusps due to following reasons:

1. The querist himself is capricornian.
2. The number as mentioned by him showed Capricorn ascendant.
3. The rising at the moment of query was Capricorn.

Therefore, from all sides the results obtained were the same. Jupiter aspects from the 5th house, therefore, I was absolutely sure that the query of the querist would be realized.

As per the traditional chart Mercury was placed in its own

sign in the 6th house. The sixth house denotes litigation, disputes, etc. the *dasa* at the time of query was Mercury *mahadasa* and Venus *bhupti*. Mercury is in the star of Rahu which is placed in the 7th house, i.e. the house of compromise and Venus is placed in the star of Moon which is also placed in the 7th house. Mercury and Venus both are in the sub of Venus, which happens to be *Rajyogakaraka* for Capricorn ascendant. Therefore, it was predicted though the case, lies before court yet it is through compromise in which both the parties are involved, would be decided. The case would be decided after Dec. 2000.

Example 6: The golden chain of a lady was stolen. She wanted to know some clues. She gave me number 27. The query was taken up for judgement on dated 13.07.2000 at 8.50 a.m. at Agra. The cusps for number 27 are as follows:

Cusp	**Sign lord**	**Star lord**	**Sub lord**
1st Cusp= 1s 7°-0'	Ven	Sun	Ketu
2nd Cusp= 2s 1°-48'	Merc	Mars	Merc
3rd Cusp= 2s 25°-48'	Merc	Jup	Ketu
4th Cusp= 3s 20°-48'	Moon	Merc	Ven
5th Cusp= 4s 20°-48'	Sun	Ven	Jup
6th Cusp= 5s 27°-48'	Merc	Mars	Jup
7th Cusp= 7s 7°-0'	Mars	Sat	Mars
8th Cusp= 8s 1°-48'	Jup	Ketu	Ven
9th Cusp= 8s 25°-48'	Jup		
		Ven	
			Merc
10th Cusp= 9s 20°-48'	Sat	Moon	Ven
11th Cusp=10s 20°-48'	Sat	Jup	Jup
12th Cusp= 11s 27°-48'	Jup	Merc	Jup.

Cuspal Chart

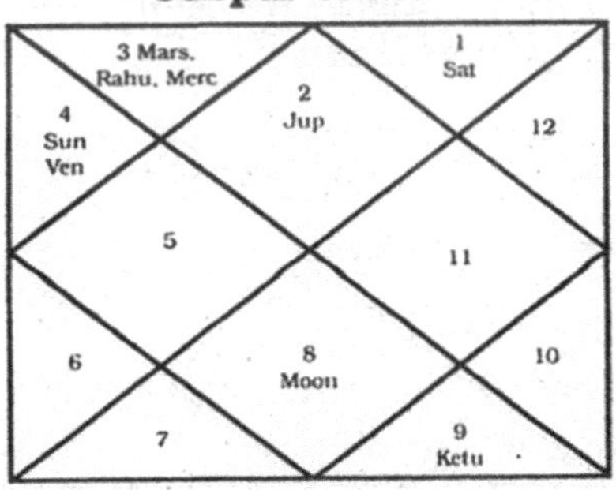

The ascendant is shown by the querist, while the 7th house is shown by the thief. The sub lord of the 7th cusp is Mercury which is placed in the 2nd house.

The 7th house is occupied by the Moon. Therefore, two female planets viz. Moon and Mercury give description of the thief. The thief must be a young and beautiful female. Since Mercury is the lord of the 2nd and 5th houses. The fifth house denotes children. Since the native does not have any daughter. Therefore, the thief may be one of the daughters in lands of the native. Since the 7th house falls in Libra sign which is ruled by Venus. When the houses—2nd, 6th and 11th are connected with each other then the stolen thing may be recevered. The sub lord of the 2nd cusp is placed in the 2nd house. The sub lord of the 6th and 11th cusps is Jupiter which is placed in ascendant. Venus, the lord of the 7th house is placed in the star of Saturn, which is placed in the 11th house (12th cusp being in the 11th house). Since Saturn is a delaying planet, therefore, there may be some delay in getting stolen chain back.

Ruling Planets:

Asd lord = Venus
Asd star lord= Sun
Moon sign lord=Mars
Moon star lord= Mer
Day ruled by = Jup.

When Moon by transit passes the area governed by these ruling planets, the stolen chain will be recovered. The *mahadasa* of Mercury and *antardasa* of Venus extends upto 17 Dec. 2001.

At the moment of query, Sun *pratyantra* was operating in Venus *bhakti* of Mercury *mahadasa*. The Sun too happens to be one of the ruling planets. Therefore, there is a probability of getting back the stolen chain.

ASTROLOGICAL STUDY OF THE GOVERNMENT—A NEW TECHNIQUE OF JUDGEMENT

Maharishi Parasara in propounding *vimshottari dasa* pattern allotted total life span to human beings was one hundred twenty years. *Vimshottari Dasa* system is widely employed to know astrologically all the events of life, which take place between one hundred twenty years. Though the average life of human being is sixty or sixty two years in India and slightly higher in other countries. It means most of the *dasas* do not even come in the life of a native.

In *Yogini Dasa* system the total life span of human beings happens to be 36 years. Thirty six years means that approximately one *dasa* once eclipsed or passed may come back in the life of the native. Since human life is full of joys and sorrows and every sorrow is followed by joy and vice versa. Therefore, how one *dasa* operates in one's life and how one *dasa* synchronises with the transit of planets with the Sun, can be studied. The mention of the Sun in this context is not irrelevant because the pathway of the Sun is uniform in the zodiac and secondly it is the significator of the soul. Therefore, the study of transit should be made in respect of the Sun too. Therefore, *Yogini Dasa* pattern seems to be logical and scientific.

In mundane astrology specially in political astrology where the astrological study is to be made in respect of government and its policies, plannings and its overall performance and downfall (death of the government) etc. must be made considering the total life span of the government to be five years (the Constitution of India allows one elected government to run for five years). In this way, the *Vimshottari Dasa* of one hundred twenty years must be reduced in proportion to the five year term of the government. Therefore, total time of the planets must be worked out accordingly.

In total the below furnishes total years or months one planet is allotted when total life span is considered to be five years.

Planets	Dasa (Years according To Vimshottari)	Dasa (Years of political Consideration)
Sun	6 years	3 months
Moon	10 years	5 months
Mars	7 years	3 months 15 days
Rahu	18 years	19 months
Jupiter	16 years	8 months
Saturn	19 years	9 months 15 days
Mercury	17 years	8 months 15 days
Ketu	7 years	3 months 15 days
Venus	20 years	10 months

Method of Working Out Dasa in Proportion of Five Years

Example: The sun has been allotted 6 years out of 120 years.

Therefore for the Sun:
120 — 6
one year gives — 6/120
five years give — 6x5/120 = 3 months and so on.
Antardasa Period:
Example: Sun based on *Vimshottari Dasa* pattern.
Antardasa of planets in the Sun *mahadasa.*

Planets	According to Vimshottari Pattern	According to new Technique
Sun	3 months 18 days	4 days 12 hours
Moon	6 months	7 days 12 hours
Mars	4 months 6 days	5 days 6 hours
Rahu	10 months 24 days	13 days 12 hours
Jupiter	9 months 18 days	12 days
Saturn	11 months 12 days	14 days 6 hours
Mercury	10 months 6 days	12 days 18 hours
Ketu	4 months 6 days	5 days 6 hours
Venus	12 months	15 days
	72 months	90 days

Method of Working out Antradasa Period in Major Period

Example: Sun *mahadasa*

(i) Sun *antardasa* operates for 3 months 18 days in 6 years *mahadasa* of the Sun in general scheme of *Vimshottari Dasa* system.

(ii) Therefore, months should be converted into days

3 months 18 days = 108 days

In 6 years of Sun *mahadasa*, the *antardasa* of the Sun operates for 108 days

or

In 2160 days of Sun *mahadasa*, the *antardasa* of the Sun operates for 108 days.

2160 — 108

one day — 108/2160

90 days, i.e. 3 months = $\frac{108 \times 90}{2160}$ = 4.5 days, i.e. 4 days

.5 x 24= 120 i.e. 12 hours = 4 days 12 hours

The other *mahadasa* and *antardasa* can also be worked out in this manner.

Next Step: Since *Vimshottari Dasa* at birth is worked out on the basis of the longitude of natal Moon. The *dasa* balance may be worked out as far as government of the country is concerned on the basis of new *dasa* system.

Example 1: Suppose Moon at any given moment was passing through *Krittika* star and the longitude was 1s 6d-10m. Taurus sign covers three pads of *Krittika* star and extends from 0d-0m to 10d-0m = 3d - 50m. It means 10d-0m-6d-10m. It means the Sun has yet to cover 3d-50m.

3d-50m or 230 minutes

The Sun covers 13 d-20m or 800 minutes in 3 months/ 800 will cover 1d or 60 m.

230 minutes will cover in 3 × 230/800 (3 months = 90 the days)

or 9 × 230/800 = 25 days 20 hours.

Similarly, *dasa* balance of the given moment of the other planets can be also be worked out.

Let us discuss some cases of coalition government and their subsequent impact on the Indian politics.

Coalition government era really began with Shri V. P. Singh (former prime minister of India) government at centre.

Example 2: Swearing in time of Shri V. P. Singh government was 12.17 noon, dated 02.12.1989, long 77 E 13, lat 28 N 19.

Sun *mahadasa* balance at swearing in time — 64 days 5 hour

i.e.

2 months 4 days 5 hours or round figure

2 months 4 days

There were two important events of Shri V. P. Singh regime.

1. Declaration of Mandal commission report leading to self immolation and chaos in the country. The report would be implemented was declared in October 90.

2. The fall of V. P. Singh government in the wake of unrest following the declaration of Mandal commission report.

Mandal commission report was declared in October 90 when Mars *dasa* was operating. Mars the lord of the 10th house was placed in the 9th house which happens to be the 12th house to the 10th house. Mars aspected not only the 12th house but also the 4th house. The 4th house denotes country and domestic happenings. Thus the malefic aspect and the lord of the 10th house clearly denoted country that foolhardy decision of the ruler could disturb the peace of the country. Mars denotes fire and devastation. Its placement, its dasa, its aspect over concerned houses were responsible for the unrest of the country.

The fall of Shri V. P. Singh government took place on dated 10th Nov 1990.

Example 3: Shri Chandrashekhar government took oath on 10th Nov. 1990 at 11.01 a.m. at New Delhi.

Ketu *mahadasa* balance - 2M 27D 3H

The Chandrashekhar government continued to remain in power from 10.11.1990 to 21.6.1991 upto Ketu *mahadasa*. Shri Chandrashekhar remained as the prime minister of India. Later on he remained caretaker prime minister till the advent of P. V. Narsimha Rao government. With the commencement of Venus *mahadasa* the government collapsed after the withdrawal of support by the Congress party. Ketu is conjoined with the lord of ascendant, i.e. Jupiter. Secondly, Ketu is placed in the star of Saturn. Saturn aspects the 10th house. Therefore, Ketu is expected to give the results of Jupiter and Saturn. Ketu provided opportunity to Shri Chandrashekhar to form the government after struggle.

In *bhava kundli* Venus is conjoined with Mercury and the Sun. Though Venus is in *mooltrikona* sign, yet it becomes malefic. Secondly, she is placed with Mercury and worst malefic for Sagittarius ascendant. In this way Venus too became malefic and brought down the government. However, Venus is considered to be a natural benefic. She conferred her benevolence as caretaker prime minister for sometime more.

Example 3: Atal Bihari Vajpayee government swearing in took place on 16.5.1996 at 12:00 noon.

Balance of Venus *mahadasa*—6M 25D 12H

Vajpayee government took oath of the office during Venus *mahadasa* and Rahu *bhukti*. Rahu *bhukti* period yet to pass remained 32 days, i.e. 1M 2D.

Venus the lord of the 3rd house and the 10th house was placed in the 11th house. The transitory moment of pleasure took place in the *bhukti* of Rahu when Vajpayee government took oath. The same Rahu *bhukti* brought down the fall of the government. Why?

1. Rahu gives unexpected gains and losses.
2. Rahu is possessed with both nectar and venom.
3. Classical texts say that Rahu gives auspicious results but it takes away everything in it's last phase.

Therefore, Rahu *bhukti* provided opportunity to Shri Vajpayee to form the government but brought down the government due to the aspect of Saturn over it. Saturn is always considered the planet of separate tendencies.

Venus though natural benefic is bound to give good results but it is also too be remembered that this planet also gives maximum results of its *mooltrikona* sign. The vary native of results largely depends upon the house being occupied by the *mooltrikona* sign. It is probably the reason that Venus is considered to be malefic even in Taurus ascendant because of its *mooltrikona* sign falling in the 6th house.

Though both *Dasa nath* and *Bhukti nath* gave moments of pleasure but soon came to their native course of effect.

Example 4: H.D. Devegowda government took oath on dated 1.6.1996 at 12.35 p.m. at New Delhi.

Balance of Saturn *mahadasa* - 5M 4D

Devegowda government collapsed on 20.4.1997. The government continued to remain in power for 10 months. It means Mercury *mahadasa* brought an end to Devegowda regime. Mercury *mahadasa* and Rahu *bhukti* finally brought down the Devegowda government. This *dasa* and *antardasa* operated from 26 March 1997 to 4 May 1997.

Rahu forms *Shadasthak* with Mercury. Mercury is placed in *Badhaksthana* with *Badhaksthanpati* lord, therefore, acts as *Badhaklord.* In *navamsa* Rahu is placed in the 10th house in the star of Moon. Moon in turn is placed in the 12th house, therefore, Rahu becomes the agent of all adverse factors with its own inherent malefic qualities which brought down the government. In *bhava lagna* too the lord of ascendant, i.e. Mercury is placed in the 8th and 3rd houses, while Rahu is placed in ascendant. Therefore, the basic foundation was quite afflicted.

A NEW APPROACH TO THE STUDY OF PRASTARASHTAK VARGA

Let me admit frankly that *asthakvarga* system of prediction really fascinated me after K.P. system of prediction. As astrologers working on the lines of K.P. (specially horary) are indeed required to look into daily positions of the planets or they take very seriously the transit of planets. I also admit it that I could not overcome my temptation to look into the transiting phase of planets and exclusively I look into *prastarashtak varga* to assess the real strength of planets (deviation from *Shadbala* method) to give results. After being finally assured by the results of planets in horary astrology even then I really look into *prastarashtak varga* to know the degree of results. It has become my habit.

I am not going to discuss the whole *asthakvarga* system of prediction nor I feel may benefit the readers as well as savant of astrology. I only intend to discuss *prastarashtak varga.*

What is *Prastarashtak* Varga? In this study each sign is divided into 8 parts. Each part consits of 3d-45m in longitude. This part is called *kaksha* and the first *kaksha* begins with Saturn. Planets placed in the *kakshas* are as per their velocities in increasing order. Therefore, the velocity of Jupiter is more than Saturn, the velocity of Mars is more than Jupiter and so on. Each planet expects Rahu and Ketu are has its own *prastarashtak varga.* In *bhinaashtakvarga* which planet has given *rekha* to which planet in which the sign is shown particularly in *prastarashtak varga.* The literal meaning of *prastarashtak* is derived from its terminology, means *prastar* i.e. expansion. The planets are shown vertically while signs are shown horizontally. The planets are in order as given below:

Saturn	—	0d-0m to 3d-45m
Jupiter	—	3d-45m to 7d-30m
Mars	—	7d-30m to 11d-15m
Sun	—	11d-15m to 15d-0m
Venus	—	15-0m to 18d-45m

Mercury — 18d-45m to 22d-30m
Moon — 22d-30m to 26d-15m
Ascendant — 26d-15m to 30d-0m

Use of *Prastarashtak* Varga: The *prastarashtak varga* is mainly used to delineate the results of the planet during transit. It is also used in electional astrology to find auspiciousness of the time. It is also employed to assess the degree of effect one planet is expected to give during its *mahadasa* or *antardasa*.

Application of *Prastarashtak* Varga: Let us understand the application of P.V. with an example.

DOB—30.04.1970
TOB—7.00 a.m.
POB—Allahabad

Let us take the example of *prastarashtak varga* of Saturn. In this P. V. Saturn in Aries sign has got *rekha* from Mars, Sun, Venus and Moon. The *kaksha* of Mars begins from 7d-30m to 11d-15m. It means when Saturn in transit passes through this longitude in Aries sign will give good results because *rekha* is associated with auspiciousness. The daily motion of Saturn is found to be fluctuating between one minute to 2 minutes (maximum). In other words, it means that Saturn roughly in 6 months passes 3d-45m. It means up to 6 to 7 months when Saturn passing through the *kaksha* of Mars will give auspicious results.

Let us look at the P. V. of the Sun. Sun in Aries sign has got *rekha* from Saturn, Sun, Venus, Moon and ascendant. The *kaksha* of Saturn begins from 0d-0m to 3d-45m. It means when the Sun passing through the *kakasha* of Saturn will give auspicious results. The daily average motion of the Sun is 1d-0m. It means for roughly four days the Sun will give good results.

Generally, the transits of Saturn, Jupiter and Mars are studied for the delineation of results because of their long stay in a particular sign. However, due to very slow motion of these planets, the time extends for quite a long time. Therefore, it is not possible on the part of astrologers to keep a vigil over the result of the planet.

Therefore, I feel some sort of modification in that general scheme of predictions so that time span may be reduced and also suitably verify the validity of the system.

Innovative Approach to the Study of P.V.

Preface: Dear readers a new idea or thought though seems at the first sight to be unscientific or unapproachable be put to test rather than on rightly rejecting it. It causes a lot of harm to the very nature of research. In the past it happened with the 'Krishnamurti Padhati'. The real losers are only astrologers because even having logic they shut their eyes from innovations and new thoughts.

In original method of K.P. there were only five ruling planets but research kept on going and the number of the ruling planets increased from five to seven. Rahu and Ketu, though not directly linked up, were also included in the list of the ruling planets.

(i) In the same direction I substituted the day lord with that of the lord of particular hora. The logic says that when the position of the planet of the given moment is taken for judgement then why to take the day lord. By substituting the day lord with that of the hora lord the results were quite amazing or at least simply hora speaks well about the querist himself.

(ii) **What is this new approach:** As regards *prastarashtak varga* I made subdivisions of *kaksha* of planets. The P.V. measures the *kaksha* of Saturn to be 3d-45m in longitude. I have further divided this kaksha and now the actual longitude of the *kaksha* of Saturn remains to be 0d-0m to 0d-28m-7s-30m. In this new system the time span is considerably reduced. In this new approach the exact timing of the event may be predicted.

Method of Calculation

Each *kaksha* extends 3d-45m in longitude.
3d-45m or 225 minutes
225/8 = 0d-28m-7"-30"' minutes
0 = degree
' = minute
" = Second
"' = Millisecond

As per subdivision of *kaksha*, the *kaksha* of Saturn appears like this

Saturn = 0d-0m to 0d-28'-7"-30"'
Jupiter = 0d-28'7"-30"' to 0d-56'-15"-0"'

Mars	=	0d-56'-15"-0"' to 1d-24'-22"30"'
Sun	=	1d-24'-22"30"' to 1d-52'30"-0"'
Venus	=	1d-52'-30"-0"' to 2d-20'-37"-30"'
Mercury	=	2d-20'-37"-30"' to 2d-48'-45"-0"'
Moon	=	2d-48'-45"-0"' to 3d-16'-52"-30"'
ASC	=	3d-16'-52"-30"' to 3d-45'-0"-0"'

In this way the *prastarashtak* of Saturn is divided into 64 parts or sub *kakshas*.

How to Proceed with These Tables

Each *kaksha* of the planets has been subdivided.

The longitude of each planet remains the same.

The longitude of each planet is given below.

Planet	Old Method	New Approach
Sat	3d-45m	0d-28'-7"-30"'
Jup	3d-45' to 7d-30'	4d-13'-7"-30"' to 4d-41'-15"-30"'
Mars	7d-30' to 11d-15'	8d-26'-15"-0"' to 8d-54'-22" -30"'
Sun	11d-15' to 15d-0'	12d-29'-22"-30"' to 13d-7'-30"-0"'
Venus	15d-0' to 18d-45'	16d-24'-22"-30"' to16d-52'-30"-0"'
Merc	18d-45' to 22d-30'	21d-33'-45"-0"' to 22d-1'-52"-30"'
Moon	22d-30' to 26d-15'	25d-18'-45"-0"' to 25d-46'-52"-30"'
ASC	26d-15' to 30d-0'	29d-31'-52"-0"' to 30-0'-0"-0"'

The longitude of subdivision of *kaksha* of any planet in any of the *prastarashtak* remains the same.

For the convenience of the readers the ready reckoner table is enclosed.

Let us Demonstrate the Case:

DOB—30.04.1970

TOB—7.00 a.m.

POB—Allahabad

In the *prastarashtak* of Venus, Venus obtains *rekha* in Taurus sign from Jupiter, Venus, Moon, Ascendant, etc. It means when Venus passes 3d-45m to 7d-30m through the *kaksha* of Jupiter will give auspicious result (old method).

In the new approach the *kaksha* of Jupiter actually begins form 14d-13'-7"-30"' to 4d-41'-15"-0"'. When Venus passes this longitude the actual result will take place.

The daily motion of Venus at an average rate is 1d-14m to

1d-16m. It means Venus will take roughly 3 days to pass 3d-45m. The Astrologers may say that within 3 days you will get good results. But in this approach the day is decided and time is also determined. As soon as on particular day Venus enters Taurus sign and passes through the *kaksha* of Jupiter (4d-13'-7"-30"' to 4d-41'-15"-0"') the native will experience good results as well as bad results as the case may be.

Take Prastarashtak of Mars: In its prastarashtak Mars has obtained *rekha* from Mars and ascendant. It means when Mars passes through the subdivided parts of the *kaksha*, i.e. 8d-26'15"-0"' to 8d-54'-22"-30"' in Taurus sign will experience the result.

The order of subdivision of *kaksha* is uniform. In *prastarashtak* of Saturn the first division begins with Saturn, similarly in the *prastarashtak* of either the Sun or Venus the first *kaksha* will always be of Saturn next to Jupiter and so on.

The utility of this approach lies in this fact that it helps the astrologer to pinpoint the time with reference to good as well as bad results.

It is important and worthy to keep it in mind that *asthakvarga* to *prastarashtak varga* is mainly employed to study the transit effect of the planet. The transit planets if do not coincide with *mahadasa* or *antardasa*, their effect upon nativity remains nil. Jupiter is going to transit Cancer sign in July 2002. Will it give its auspicious result to all and sundry? No, the native having either *mahadasa* or *antardasa* of Jupiter will experience the results. The degree of effect depends upon the *prastarashtak* of Jupiter.

Conclusion: Esteemed readers and savants of astrology are requested to verify this new approach of prediction.

SUBDIVISION TABLE OF *KAKSHA*

SATURN-0d-0m to 3d-45m

Sat = 0d-0, to 28d-7'-30"
Jup =0d-28'-7"-30''' to 0d-56'-15"-0'''
Mars=0d-56'-15"-0''' to 1d-24'-22"-30'''
Sun=1d-24'-22"-30''' to 1d-52'30"-0'''
Venus=1d-52'-30"-0''' to 2d-20'-37"-30'''
Merc=2d-20'-37"-30''' to 2d-48'-45"-0'''
Moon=2d-48'-45"-0''' to 3d-16'-52"-30'''
Asc=3d-16'-52"-30''' to 3d-45'-0"-0'''

JUPITER-3d-45 to 7d-30m

Sat=3d-45'-0"-0" to 4d-13'-7"30'''
Jup=4d-13'-7"-30''' to 4d-41'-15"-0'''
Mars=4d-41'-15"-0''' to 5d-9'-22"-30'''
Sun=5d-9'-22"-30''' to 5d-31'-30"-0'''
Venus=5d-31'-30"-0''' to 6d-5'-37"-30'''
Merc=6d-5'-37"-30''' to 6d-33'-45"-0'''
Asc=7d-1'-52"-30''' to 7-30'-0"-0'''

MARS-7d-30m to 11d-15m

Sat=7d-30'-0"-0''' to 7d-58'-7"-30'''
Jup=7d-58'-7"-30''' to 8d-26'-15"-0'''
Mars=8d-26'-15"-0''' to 8d-54'-22"-30'''
Sun=8d-54'-22"-30''' to 9d-22'-30"-0'''
Venus=9d-22'-30"-0''' to 9d-50'-37"-30'''
Merc=9d-50'-37"-30''' to 10d-18'-45"-0'''
Moon=10d-18'-45"-30''' to 10d-46'-52"-30'''
Asc=10d-46'-52"-30''' to 11d-15'-0"-0'''

SUN-11d-15' to 15d-0"

Sat=11d-15'-0"-0" to 11d-43'-7"-30'''
Jup=11d-43'-7"-30''' to 12d-11'-15"-0'''
Mars=12d-11'-15"-0''' to 12d-39'-22"-30'''
Sun=12d-39'-22"-30''' to 13d-7'-30"-0'''
Venus=13d-7'-30"-0''' to 13d-35'-37"-30'''
Merc=13d-35'-37"-30''' to 14d-3'-45"-0'''
Moon=14d-3'-45"-0''' to 14d-31'-52"-30'''
Asc=14d-31'-52"-30''' to 15d-0'-0"-0'''

VENUS-15d-0m to 18d-45m

Sat =15d-0'-0"-0''' to 15d-28'-7"-30'''
Jup = 15d-28'-7"-30''' to 15d-56'-15"-0'''
Mars=15d-56'15"-0''' to 16d-24'-22"-0'''
Sun=16d-24'-22"-30''' to 16d-52'-30"-0'''
Venus=16d-52'-30"-0''' to 17d-20'-37"-30'''
Merc=17d-20'-37"-30''' to 17d-48'-45"-0'''
Moon=17d-48'-45"-0''' to 18d-16'-52"-30'''
Asc=18d-16'-52"-30''' to 18d-45'-0"-0'''

MERCURY-18d-45m to 22d-30'm

Sat=18d-45'-0"-0''' to 19d-13'-7"-30'''
Jup=19d-13'-7"-30''' to 19d-41'-15"-0'''
Mars=19d-41'-15"-0''' to 20d-9'-22"-30'''
Sun=20d-9'-22"-30''' to 20d-31'-30"-0'''
Venus=20d-31'-30"-0''' to 21d-5'-37"-0'''
Merc=21d-5'-37"-30''' to 21d-33'-45"-0'''
Moon=21d-33'-45"-0''' to 22d-1'-52"-30'''
Asc=22d-1'-52"-30''' to 22d-30'-0"-0'''

MOON-22d-30m to 26d-15m

Sat=22d-30'-0"-0''' to 22d-58'-7"-30'''
Jup=22d-58'-7"-30''' to 23d-26'-15"-0'''
Mars=23d-26'-15"-0''' to 23d-54'-22"-30'''
Sun=23d-54'-22"-30''' to 24d-22'-30"-0'''
Venus=24d-22'-30"-0''' to 24d-50'-37"-0'''
Merc=24d-50'-37"-0''' to 25d-18'-45"-0'''
Moon=25d-18'-45"-0''' to 25d-46'-52"-30'''
Asc=25d-46'-52"-30''' to 26d-15'-0"-0'''

ASCENDANT- 26d-15m to 30d-0'

Sat-26d-15'-0"-0''' to 26d-43'-7"-30'''
Jup=26d-43'-7"-30''' to 27d-11'-15"-0'''
Mars=27d-11'-15"-0''' to 27d-39'-22"-30'''
Sun=27d-39'-22"-30''' to 28d-7'-30"-0'''
Venus=28d-7'-30"-0''' to 28d-35'-37"-30'''
Merc=28d-35'-37"-30''' to 29d-3'-45"-0'''
Moon=29d-3'-45"-0''' to 29d-31'-52"-0'''
Asc=29d-31'-52"-0''' to 30d-0'-0"-0'''

FEW FUNDAMENTAL PRINCIPLES OF ASTROLOGY

Nobody can say with certainty what will happen at the next moment. The only thing which is certain is uncertainty. The human quest to know future events not only rests at astrology but all science viz. physics, astronomy, chemistry, etc. made progress due to underline quest of human beings to know future events. The research made in all sciences whether it is physics or astromony and their subsequent results only show relative truth or in broad sense principles given so far are mere hypothesis and astrology too is not an exception. However, the difference between research of physics and astrology is that, in former case, research begins with the exterior world and ends even at the exterior world. While in later case though research begins with the exterior world but ends at the interior world, i.e. in astrology intuitive kind of knowledge plays its major role rather than rational knowledge. One of the major reasons of predictions go wrong it is when intuitive knowledge is expressed through language. The pure intuitive nature of knowledge is lost and the medium of expression itself acts as an error of keyboard. Therefore, in order to make snapshot predictions astrologers must resort only to intuition. When they have highly developed intuitive power only then planets unfold their mystery before them. Therefore, it is advised that astrologers must be devotees of some god or goddess.

Though research in astrology helped in understanding the principles of astrology but also able to put up few principles which are quite valid in a number of cases though exceptions may also persist. I would like to present the following two important factors:

1. Exception does not make a rule.
2. The behaviour of planets is always mysterious.

If any of the fundamental principles of astrology is violated by an exception it does not confirm that the principle is not valid. Secondly, it is very difficult or a riddle for the astrologers to pinpoint the exact behaviour of the planets. Sometime it has been observed that the benefic planet may turn out to be the worst malefic. In what particular manner a planet will behave is the real problem of astrology.

As a humble student of astrology and being in the field for the long time I have observed some valid principles of astrology, I present, few of them for the benefit of readers:

Rahu: The placement of Rahu either in the 3rd house or eleventh house makes the native to be either the youngest or the eldest in the family.

The Lord of Ascentand: If the lord of ascendant is placed in the 3rd house the native in his unconsciousness has deep attachments for his blood relatives viz parents, brother & sisters etc.

Rahu-Moon: This conjunction gives dual personality and the native is obstinate by nature. This conjunction also associates the native, once at any stage of life, to public service.

Rahu-Moon-Mercury: The native is a lunatic and perverted by nature. The triplicity at once reveals the mental make up of the native.

Mercury: Mercury in the 4th house not in own sign once brings break down in education though favourable aspect over this house by benefics may help in resuming education.

Venus: Venus in the 4th house gives a number of vehicles to the native. If Venus is exalted or occupies own sign then excellent vehicles are enjoyed by the native.

Saturn-Moon Opposition: Moon and Saturn in mutual aspect causes delay in marriage or this combination causes such conditions which may put the entire marriage ceremony at stake.

Jupiter-Moon Opposition: The combination of elopement or love marriage.

Scorpio Ascendant and the Role of mars and Jupiter:

1. If Mars aspects the ascendant the native is very hot tempered.

2. If Mars aspects ascendant and the birth *rasi* happens to be Sagittarius, the native is not only hot tempered but also have acid tongue.

3. Jupiter is in Scorpio ascendant rules over the 5th and second houses, therefore, becomes *yogakaraka*.

4. If Jupiter is placed in the 5th house, i.e. in his own

sign, gives excellent results but turns out to be a malefic in last place of his *dasa*. The reason is, during Jupiter *mahadasa* if Jupiter is placed in the 5th house, aspects the 11th house and the 9th house, gives good results. But his lordship over the house also causes troubles in the last phase of Jupiter *mahadasa* because the 2nd house acts as *Marakslhana* and Jupiter having its *mooltrikona* sign in the 2nd house and gives results of the 2nd house more severely because of his *mooltrikona* sign. Though Jupiter, in last phase, may not cause death of the native.

Note: It may also happen that in the first phase of Jupiter *mahadasa* bad results may occur. This happens only when Jupiter is placed in the 9th house because 9th house happens to be the 8th house to the 2nd house and every planet predominantly gives first the results of his *mooltrikona* sign.

Taurus Ascenmdant: 1. Though Saturn is said to be the best benefic for this ascendant yet also acts as *badhaksthanapati* lord. Therefore, it is not fully bestowed to give good results. It is that particular ascendant in which Saturn, Mercury and the Sun are placed together. The *mahadasa* of any one out of three planets may give excellent boost to the native.

2. If two planets out of three are placed together and the third one aspects them, even then excellent results are obtained irrespective of any *bhava* they occupy.

If the lord of ascendant is placed in the 9th house or the lord of the 9th house is placed in ascendant the native once goes to foreign.

Mars-Saturn conjunction makes the native inclined towards disputes and forgery, i.e. one has natural tendency for cheating and forgery.

Transit of Saturn—A Few Observations

1. **Scorpio Ascendant:** Saturn being the lord of the 3rd and 4th houses respectively in Aries sign which falls in the 6th house, causes a lot of troubles to the youngest brother of the native. If the *dasha* of Saturn is also operating at the time of Saturn's stay in the Aries sign it will create a lot of trouble to one of the younger brothers of the native.

Example: DOB-27.07.1943 TOB 2 p.m., POB Gunna (M.P.)

The brother of the native got fractured in his back bone in May 2000 and was admitted to the hospital in a serious condition. The Saturn as per birth chart of the native was placed in the 6th house being the lord of the 3rd and 4th houses. The debilitated Saturn caused trouble to the brother of the native.

Example: DOB 31.03.1940 TOB 11p.m., POB Agra (U.P.)

The younger brother of the native first suffered from tuberculosis and later on died in a tragic accident. Both the events happened in May and June 2000. The brother of the native died as soon as Saturn transited Taurus sign. It is interesting to note that Saturn is placed in the 6th house in natal chart and the native suffered due to her younger brothers. It was transiting Saturn over natal Saturn which brought ultimate end to the one of the younger brothers.

Note: In the above two cases discussed Saturn's stay in Aries sign caused trouble to the younger brothers but not their death. It is only after Saturn's entry into Taurus that brought the end to the younger brother of the native no. 2. The fate of the brother of the Ex. no. 1 is not known to me till the writing of this article.

2. **Sagittarius Ascendant**: Saturn in Aries in the 5th house aspects the 11th house which happens to be the 8th house to the 4th house causes deterioration of the health of the mother.

Example: DOB 2.08.1966 TOB 4.20 p.m. POB Agra (U.P.)

Saturn's stay in the 5th house in Aries sign and its aspect over the 11th house caused serious ailments like diabetes to mother because the 11th house happens to be the 8th house to the 4th house—the seat of mother. The native herself got separation form her husband because from the 5th house Saturn aspects the 7th house.

3. **Capricorn Ascendant**: When Saturn transits Taurus sign in June 2000 and stays there in for two years and a half may be a serious concern for the mother of the native. Therefore, native must resort to *shani shaman* for the well being of mother. It may also create health problems for the wife of the native.

Saturn, also hampers the health of mother because the 4th house is the seat of mother. Saturn in debilitation in the 4th house affected the health of mother.

Saturn, now in Taurus sign, aspects the 11th house which

happens to be 8th house to the 4th house. Therefore, this time may not be favourable to the mother of native.

4. **Gemini Ascendant:** As soon as Saturn transited Taurus sign the native was put behind the bars. He remained in Jail for ten days. Rahu as per transit was placed in the 2nd house and Saturn in transit occupies the 12th house. Thus ascendant comes into the effect of *Papakartri Yoga.* Neeraj Jyotish Dhoavali vides its *Sloka* no. 32 to explain it elaborately.

Example: DOB 12.10.1972, TOB 10.55 p.m., POB Agra

5. **Cancer Ascendant**: The Saturn is considered to be functional malefic for Cancer ascendant. During its stay in 10th house in Aries sign from ascendant delayed her marriage but in the last phase of its stay in Aries sign cleared her marriage prospects. As soon as Saturn transited Taurus sign she got married. Saturn during its stay in Aries sign was in debilitation, therefore, though aspecting its own sign in 7th house was not able to accrue favourable results. As soon as it switched over to friendly sign-Taurus, it gave marriage to the Native.

Example: DOB 3.071972, TOB 6.55 a.m., POB Lucknow

6. **Leo Ascendant**: Saturn stay in the 9th house in Aries sign from ascendant causes havoc in the married life of the native. In the last phase the native was badly beaten and ousted form home in the midnight by her husband. Married life at present is at the brink of collapse. However, Saturn's transited in Taurus sign may not cause divorce because from the 10th house Saturn aspects its own *mooltrikona* sign which falls in the 7th house of the native (As predicted by me to the father of native),

Example: DOB 9.8.1962, TOB 7.55 a.m., POB Kanauj (U.P.)

7. **Virgo Ascendant**: As soon as Saturn transited Taurus sign, i.e. in the 9th house from ascendant the younger brother of the father of the native died. Saturn aspects the 11th house which happens to be the 3rd to the 9th house denoting younger brother of the father of the native.

Example: DOB 12.09.1971, TOB 7.00 a.m., POB Agra.

SPIRITUAL ACHIEVEMENTS

I remember the function held in FICCI Golden Jubilee auditorium hall New Delhi where Late R. Santhanam award was to be declared. I also delivered a lecture on astrology. During my lecture I emphasized the role of Jupiter, Saturn and Venus in developing intuition power which is necessary for astrological perceptions. The astrologers participated in the function would be in agreement with me on the mention of Jupiter and Saturn because both the planets are directly or indirectly related with the development of soul. However, the mention of Venus in the development of intuition power may sound awkward to them because Venus has always been linked up with the luxury and sexual conception of life.

Our ancient seers had advocated *Hath Yoga* and *Sahaja Yoga*. *Hath Yoga* is achieved through the depression and subjugation of desires, while *Sahaj Yoga* is achieved through the absolute fulfillment of desires. In both the cases the ultimate aim of *yoga* is the cessation of all desires. When desires ceases to exist meditation rises which is the beginning of intuition. *Hath Yoga* is supplemented by Jupiter and especially by Saturn, the planet of sufferings, while *Sahaj Yoga* is supplemented by Venus. *Hath Yoga* is the negation of all desires while *Sahaja Yoga* is the acceptance of all desires. Indian philosophy represents two classical examples of above two *yogas*. Bhagwan Mahaveer represents the sect of *Hath Yoga* while Budh represents the sect of *Sahaja Yoga*. To achieve this state of *yoga* the essential condition lies in the fact one should not have even the perception of desire. Desire gives rises to ego while ego generates anger and anger spoils the reason (*vivek*). Which, ultimately, brings destruction of human personality.

In one of his famous books 'Sex to Super Consciousness' Acharya Rajnesh (OSHO) emphasized bliss in the attainment of *samadhi* or superconciousness provided the human being must change the direction of energy from outside to inner side with such *Anand* what he or she experienced during sexual union. In nutshell he propagated *Sahaj Yoga*. While I mentioned Venus in developing intuition power I had kept such things in mind apart the other qualities of Venus.

In Greece mythology Venus is considered to be the goddess of beauty. Beauty cannot be judged from rational point of view, it can be only perception which can be judged at the level of soul. Therefore, beauty is linked up with the soul. Venus gives rise to emotion, pity, humanness, imagination, sympathy, love, etc. all these qualities are naturally incorporated into human personalities are termed as innate qualities of human beings. Such qualities are nothing but the manifestation of soul in proportion to the development of soul in the incarnation concerned. If Venus is branded as the planet of bed comforts and all kinds of luxury in life, I safely vouch that such things must be developed to the saturation point because from the saturation point further flow of energy turns its direction. The unafflicted and strong Venus develops such innate qualities which bring human being near to its inner consciousness.

The houses of spiritual development are mainly the 5th and 9th house and the 2nd house. The 5th house deals with divine knowledge while the 9th house deals with *dharma* and house of balancing view of life because this house blends *bhagya* with *dharma*, i.e. matter and spirit. The 2nd house represents voice. The impressive voice is required for the dissemination of spiritual knowledge. Therefore, this house also should be strong. The 12th house has not been included because the 12th house is considered to be *moksha sthana*, i.e. final liberation from the cycle of birth and death. Here we have to examine the spiritual manifestation in respect of material world.

Spiritual achievements can manifest in a number of forms viz. *yogis*, artists, poets, philosophers, astrologers, social reformers, politicians, etc. It is to be worth mentioning here that any special progress in any particular field or above mentioned roles reflect that the incarnation is endowed with some special qualities. Spiritual achievements have not been taken literary where it is linked with *dhyani* or *gyani* (mediator or learned). Through this paper this particular connotation has been enlarged encompassing all the persons who had/ have achieved distinctions in their field of action. Let us discuss a combination for spiritual achievements as mentioned in the classical texts:

Doctrines of Sukh Nadi—Translation by Late R. Santhanam

1. There will be spiritual achievements galore if the lord of the ascendant the 9th and the 12th house join in the angle of, in aspect of Jupiter.

2. If the lords of the 8th and 10th houses counted from the ascendant join together in the 9th sign counted from the Moon and be in aspect to Venus.

3. The following planetary *yoga* will also produce the same effect if the 10th lord is in exaltation. Saturn in the ascendant as the Moon in the 9th house with Jupiter.

4. Should Venus be in the ascendant and aspect Saturn again spiritual achievements will be in galore.

5. The native will be well versed in *saivism* and be a famous propagator of the said school of thought if the lords of the ascendant, the 4th and 5th join in the 2nd in aspect of Jupiter.

6. The same results will be experienced if the planets viz. rulers of the ascendants the 5th, 7th and 9th join in the 9th aspect of Jupiter.

Other classical texts on astrology provide other combinations too. Keeping in view above statements the following charts have been discussed.

Example 1: 15.08.1872 at 5.17 a.m. (L.M.T), (Lat 22D-30N' Long 88D-20'E)

This example has been taken from Late Dr. B. V. Raman's famous book 'Notable Horoscopes'. Charts belong to Aurbindo Ghose. The life of Aurbindo Ghose is a classical example of transformation of self into divinity. The journey of his life

Natal Chart

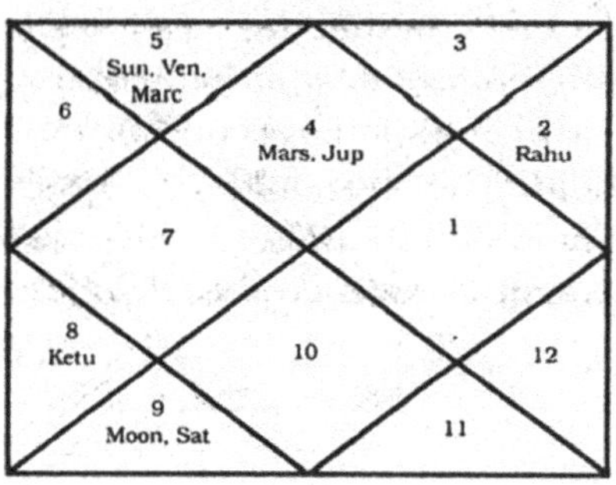

Navamsa

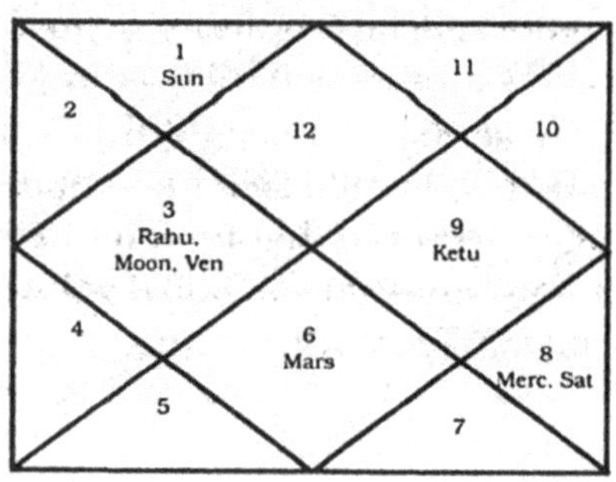

started from gun cult and ended in 'Savitri'. His association with revolutionist, during India's freedom struggle, forced him to join extremist group of freedom fighters. He took gun to liberate India from colonial rule. From philosophical point of view the trust in gun cult showed his fear of death, while 'Savitri' (his famous epic) showed his efforts how to get victory over death and are two phenomenal aspects of his life.

The ascendant lord joins Saturn in the 6th house, prepares the mind of the native to be philosophical. The aspect of Jupiter over the 5th and 9th houses shows the element of divinity to be in subdued stage. The formation of *Budh-Aditya Yyoga* in the 2nd house and placement of Venus there in makes one learned and bestows on beautiful and impressive voice. The lord of the 5th house is debilitated. Thus the house of divine knowledge, i.e. the 5th house was not affected due to Mars or Mars producing qualities. However, the placement of Mars in ascendant with Jupiter gave rise to a personality who was mission oriented. Fire and energy of Mars got transformed into specific goal of life which resulted in the generation of patriotic feelings in the native. As I said above the divinity in initial stage in Aurbindo's life was in subdued state because Mars the *rajyogkarka* was playing his role which prepared the native to take up gun for the country. Here it also be noted that debilitated 5th house lord and unblemished aspect of Jupiter over the 5th house clearly reveals that when the role of *rajyogkarka* is over, starts the role of *yogkarka* which happens to be Jupiter. His real *yogi* life began during the *mahadasa* of Rahu. Rahu is in Taurus sign ruled by Venus. Thus Venus provided ample imagination and changed the direction of his consciousness to the inner word. The study of Venus is very important in his case. Venus is placed in the 2nd house along with the Sun and Mercury. Mercury reduced the sexual qualities of Venus where as the placement of Sun with Venus increases the qualities of Venus. Thus it can be deduced of Venus on the other hand the sun increases the fine qualities of Venus though Venus is said to be afflicted, it changes the direction of energy of Aurbindo at a higher level of consciousness. Venus is afflicted, therefore, it brought mother a French lady to Aurbindo's *ashram*. Venus prepared Aurbindo to dwell into high realms of consciousness, therefore, his relationship with mother was untained and remained platonic one. Thus from the horoscope of Aurbindo the role of Saturn, Jupiter and Venus can be easily understood in the development of higher level of consciousness. Readers would be pleased to note that in case of Aurbindo the consciousness developed further to become superconsiousness and Aurbindo reached the *Sakshi Bhava* (the state of being witness only) of *Samkhya Darshan.*

Example 2: 2.10.1869 at 7:45 P.M. (L.M.T) (Lat 21D-37' N Long 69D-49'E)

Natal Chart

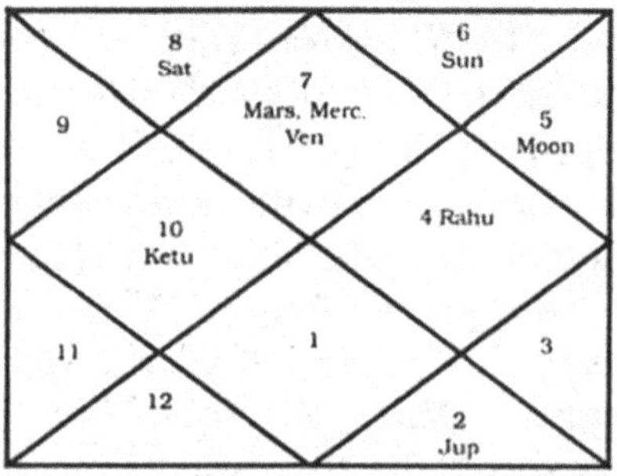

Navamsa

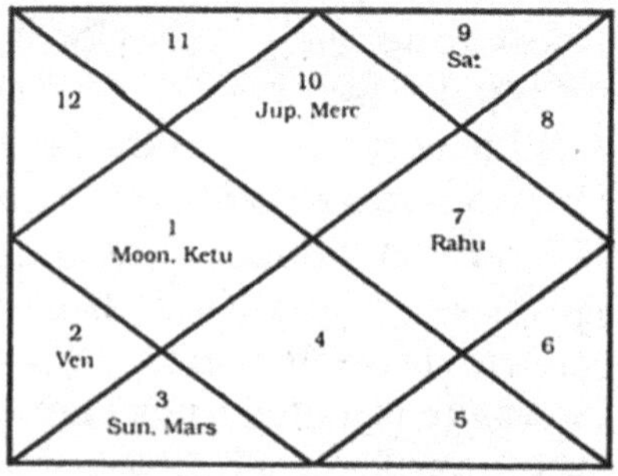

This example has been taken from 'Notable Horoscopes' by Dr. B. V. Raman.

This horoscope belongs to father of nation Late M. K. Gandhi. Like former example of Aurbindo Ghose the case of Mahatma Gandhi is also the classical example of spirituality arising out of humdrum political life.

The involvement of Mahatma Gandhi in politics was due to his sensitivity towards the misery of people. His notion of life was basically derived from the sufferings and self-respect of the people of his country. There are also two distinct features of his life:

1. His involvement in India's polity during India's struggle for freedom.
2. His philosophical ideas for restructuring India.

The placement of Mars, Venus and Mercury in ascendant made him intelligent, learned and man of unusual sexual likings. In his famous book 'My Experiments with Truth', he himself admitted the fact that he was quite sexual person. The placement of two contradictory planets, i.e. Mars and Mercury with Venus was clear cut testimony that one day at the cost of sexual life other more constructing channels would open before him. The influence of Mars, Venus, Jupiter and Saturn over the 4th house, the house of emotions and practical knowledge, gave indication about the emotional level and practical knowledge of Gandhi. As I have said earlier in the preface of this article that emotion is the attribute of soul. Thus it was his emotion which turned him from barrister to a man of humanity. The horoscope of Gandhi clearly depicts the role of Venus in the transcendental development of soul or the attributes of soul. In *navamsa* the 5th house is influenced by Venus and Jupiter while the 2nd, house in natal chart is influenced by Saturn and Jupiter. The aspect of Jupiter over the house of speech, i.e. the 2nd house makes one good orator while Saturn in this house makes the person to speak with caution.

It was the farsightedness of Gandhi coupled with practical knowledge that he introduced many experiments in Indian politics. Religion based politics, and propagation of *Ahimsa* in Indian politics are such examples. It is his spirituality that without any vested interest he served the country. It was his spirituality that tears dropped from his eyes even at the death of his opponents or enemies.

Note: 1. The 4th house represents practical knowledge and emotions. While the 5th house represents divine knowledge.

2. For more detailed qualities of Mars-Venus, Mercury-Venus please see article A New Approach to Matching of Charts.

Example 3: DOB 14.04.623 B.C. at about mid day (Lat 27D-8' Long 83' -5' E). Example taken from 'Notable Horoscopes'.

Natal Chart

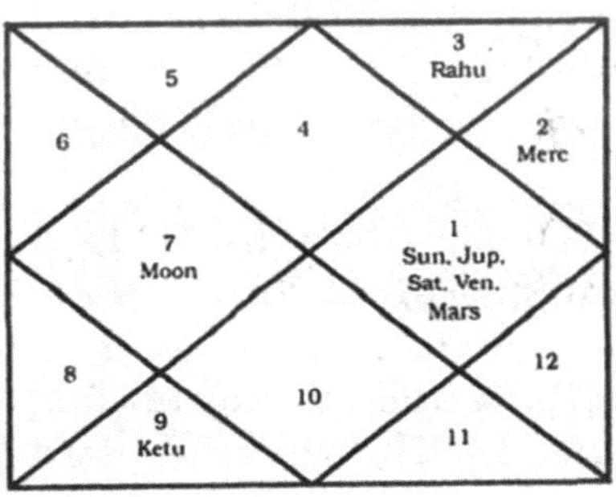

Navamsa

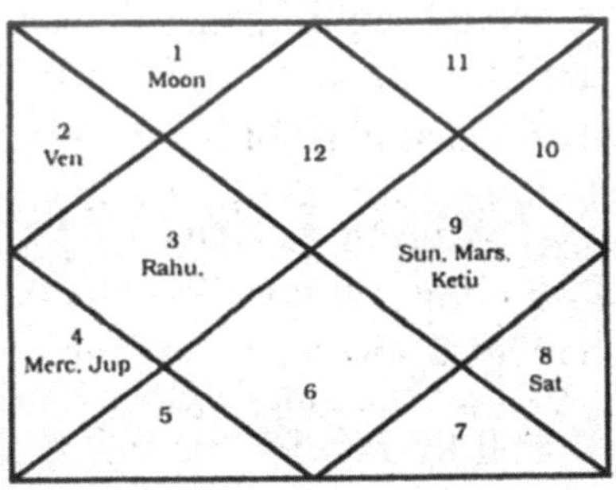

This horoscope belongs to Gautam Budha. The first sight look of the horoscope reveals the presence of *Parivrajak Yoga* in the horoscope. The most important fact of this horoscope is that almost all the planets aspect the 4th house, the house of emotion. It is well known fact that emotions played a turning point in the life of Gautam and awakened his slumbering soul, therefore, he was called Budha, i.e. who is awakened. The placement of the 5th and 9th lords in the 10th with Venus, Saturn and the Sun changed the flow of energy from the exterior world to the interior world of deep consciousness. The aspect of almost all the planets on the significator of mind, i.e. Moon showed that mind was under the dominating influence of all the planets and was also affected due to increased level of emotion and ultimately mind lost for the manifestation of soul. The aspect of Jupiter over the 2nd house adorns Budha with impressive magnificent voice which helped him to convince people about the great reality of life. The placement of Moon in Libra sign aspected by Saturn gave him magnetic appearance. There are two important houses viz. 4th and 10th which in association with the 5th and 9th houses exert their influence on the personality and outlook of Budha. Emotion, sympathy, kindness, generosity (4th house) and house of deeds (10th house) influence each other which manifested in the great teachings of Budha putting emphasis on the specific attribute of the soul, i.e. *karuna* or *kindness. karuna* or kindness (though kindness is not synonyms of *karuna*) is generated only when one reflects his image in others. Such a state of thinking is achieved when the person starts experiencing the attribute of soul which are nothing but the manifestation of divinity in various forms.

Note: Though the 4th house is not directly related with the spiritual achievements yet it generates and helps in the manifestation of attributes of soul to that level where the mediation of the fifth or ninth houses becomes insignificant.

Example 4: DOB 7.05.1861 POB 2.51 a.m. (L. M. T) (Lat. 22D-40'N, Long 88'-30'N). Example taken from 'Notable Horoscopes'.

The horoscope belongs to Late Rabindranath Tagore. Tagore is well known for his spiritual writings. The ascendant lord is exalted in the 5th house arousing, deep insight and intuition power. The *Budh-Aditya Yoga* made him intelligent and learned, while Venus turned this *yoga* into fine sensitive imaginations which resulted in the literary works like 'Gitanjali'. The placement of Venus in the 2nd house and the aspect of Jupiter over the 2nd house bestowed on him sweet, spiritual and melodious voice. In *navamsa* the placement of Rahu, Sun and Venus made him sensitive by nature and produced natural urge of humanity in him as this house was also aspected by Jupiter. Thus these two planets, viz. Venus and Jupiter were able to change the direction of energy to creative and spiritual writings.

Natal Chart

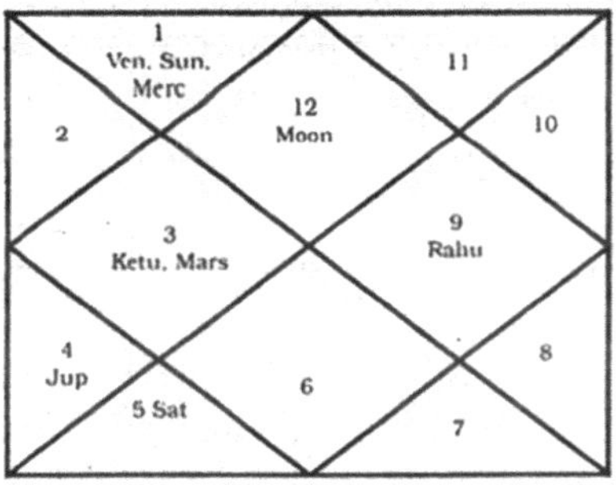

Navamsa

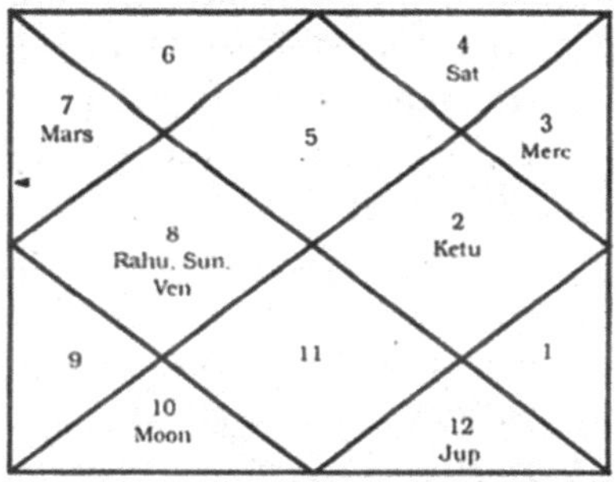

Note: The placement of sun in the 4th house either in natal chart or *navamsa* makes one bereft of any emotional attachment to the persons he is surrounded. Please see the placement of Mars in natal chart in the fourth house being the lord of the ninth house and the Sun in the fourth house in the *navamsa*. The placement of Mars being the lord of the 2nd and 9th houses on one side evoked the spirit of detached attachment and on the other side prepared the native to construct the centre of education like 'Shanti Niketan'. The Sun also increased the spirit of detached attachment which had been necessary for him as attachment which had been necessary for him as attachment creates barrier in the way of self realization.

Example 5: DOB 29/30.07.1930, TOB 3:18 a.m., POB Gwalior

This case is slightly different from the above cases. The

native belongs to erstwhile M. P. known as Pahargarh. Though the state was not granted statehood due to political reasons, yet this state enjoyed full- fledged independence. The native Kunwar Padam Singh belongs to *kshatriya* clan and was brought up in royal atmosphere which is expected to be prevalent in royal and *kshatriya* families. The education of this man was poor as the native did not show any sign of interest towards learning and education.

The man entered into public life about thirty-five years ago and at present, is the chairman of a co-operative bank.

This man showed a remarkable transformation from material to spiritual life. The man who used to believe in gun cult became admirer of books and knowledge. This can be judged from the fact that he is also an astrologer and shows a keen interest in astrology and other divine knowledge. What allures me to study his chart are the following reasons:

1. Transformation of his soul from arrogance to submissiveness.

2. Though he is not educated yet his interest in divine knowledge is remarkable.

3. He has good grasping power and is possessed with practical knowledge necessary to run financial institution like banking.

The placement of Jupiter in ascendant is said to be the best position as at this position the directional strength of Jupiter is said to be one *rupa*. Jupiter aspects the 5th and 9th houses. Both houses are related with secret knowledge and *dharma bhava* respectively. In *navamsa*, the ascendant is Capricorn which is said to be a mystic sign of Zodiac and sign of saints, philosophers. Thus it may be assumed that philosophical seeds were present in dormant stage in him. Thus Jupiter, which aspects the 5th and 9th houses, clears the dust lying over his soul. Saturn's aspect over Jupiter not only adds philosophy in divinity but also makes one a politician from his actions and thoughts.

Budh-Aditya Yoga in the 2nd house not only makes him very sweet in speaking but endows him to possess practical knowledge which he utilizes in his day to day functioning.

In *navamsa*, Saturn aspects the 5th house, Jupiter and Saturn have mutual aspects. Thus, this sort of planetary configuration brought radical change in his outlook towards

Natal Chart

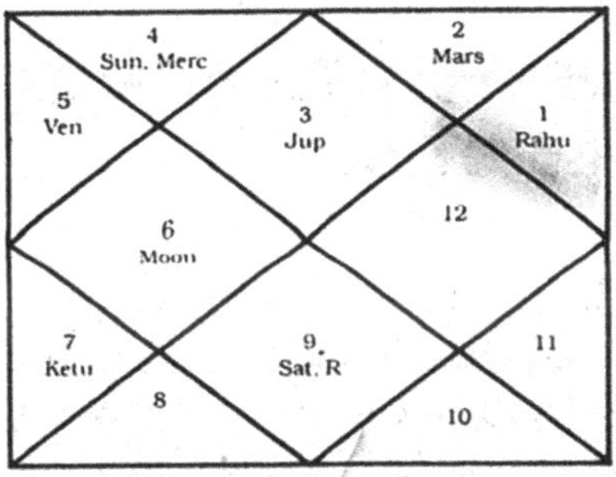

Navamsa

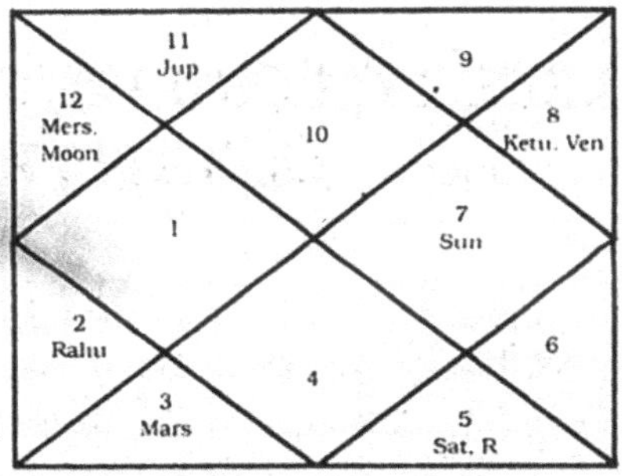

life. The esteemed editor of the 'Times of Astrology' rightly observed while making commentary on *Lomesh Samhita* that the placement of *Lagnesh* in the 2nd house person will be well behaved as well as gainful out of his/her behaviour. It is the behaviour of this person that he is able to subdue any revolt arising out of political compulsions. It is his behaviour which helped him to hold the post of the chairman for the last 19 years inspite of criticism and revolt.

ROLE OF LORD OF CONSTELLATION AND SUB IN PREDICTIONS

Late K. S. Krishnamurty was a pioneer in developing predictions based on the lord of Constellation and sub. Sub in the 9th part of a constellation. The longitude of a constellation is 13°-20' which is uniform for every constellation. The longitude of sub is in accordance with the years allotted to a planet in *vimshattari Dasa* system. Therefore, the longitude of a sub varies from planet to planet as the years allotted to each planet in *vimshattari Dasa* varies. But the same where years are also same viz Mars and Ketu.

Sub	**Longitued**
Moon	1°-6'-40"
Sun	0°-40'-0"
Mars	46°-0'-40"
Ven	2°-13'-20"
Merc	1°-55'-20"
Sat	2°-6'-20"
Rahu	2°-0'-0"
Ketu	0°-46'-40"
Jup	1°-46'-40"

In predictive astrology, when the position of a planet along with the position of constellation lord in which planet is posited is taken into account, the results are more promising. Nobody can doubt the fundamentals and principles regarding the planetary position in a horoscope as laid down by our ancient sages. But blindly adhering to these rules may lead to failure in predictions, questioning the authenticity of astrology as a whole. Therefore, Late K. S. Krishnamurty along with the fundamental rules of astrology, added with the theory of constellation and sub, made a new headway in astrology. Although the greater utility of sub is to be found in horary astrology. But its importance in reaching definite conclusion in prediction in natal astrology is also noteworthy.

According to Krishnamurty, planet during its *dasa* and *bhukti* offers the results of lord of constellation in which the planet is situated more predominantly along with its position in the horoscope and its aspect on the other houses.

Example 1: Born on 17.11.1961 at 11.05 a. m. at Agra
Birth star— Poorva Padrapada
Balance of Jupiter *mahadasa* at birth = 11Y 6M 21D

		Star	**Lord**	**Sub lord**
Ascendant	= 9s 1°-55'	uttara Sada	Sun	Jup
Sat	= 9s 1°-55'	uttara Sada	Sun	Jupiter
Jup	= 9s 8°-28'	Uttara Sada	Sun	Venus
Mars	= 7s 9°-4'	Anurada	Sat	Venus
Sun	= 7s 14°-10'	Vishaka	Jup	Mars
Ven	= 6s 14°-11'	Swati	Rahu	Merc
Merc	= 6s 15°-24'	Swati	Rahu	Ven
Moon	= 10s 23°-42'	Poorvapadrapada	Jup	Sat
Rahu	= 3s 29°-10'	Ashlesa	Merc	Sat
Ketu	= 9s 29°-10'	Dhanistha	Mars	Sat

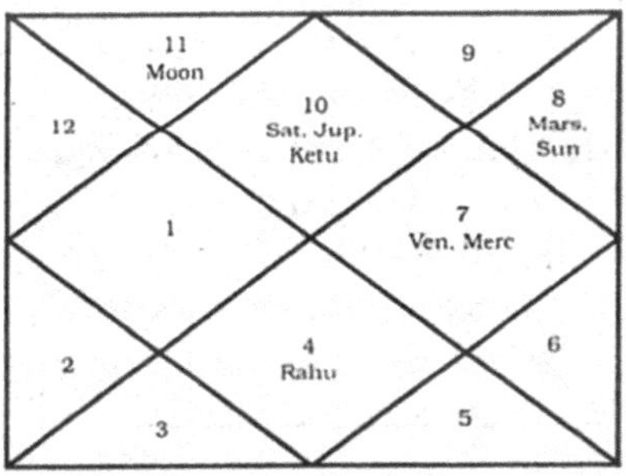

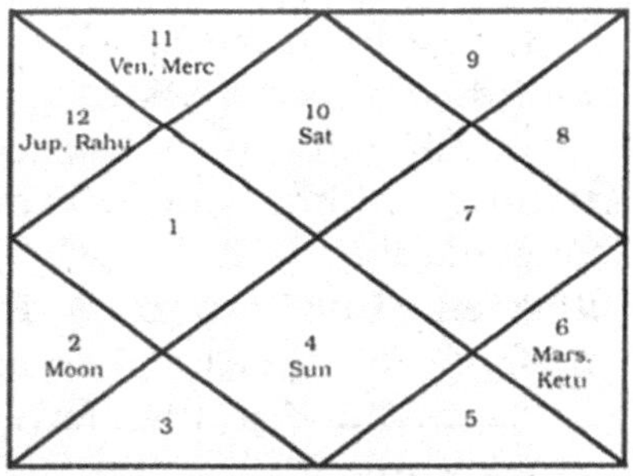

Native joined the service on dated 4.8.1984 when he was running saturn *mahadasa*, Moon *bhukti* and Sun *antardasa*. Saturn was in the constellation of the Sun and in the sub of Jupiter. The Moon was in the constellation of Jupiter and the sub of Saturn. the Sun was in the constellation of Jupiter and in the sub of Mars.

Therefore, the planets viz. Saturn, Moon and the Sun were to give the results of lord of constellation viz. Sun, Jupiter, Mercury and Mars. They, of course, gave results. Saturn and Jupiter are placed into ascendant, Mercury in the 10th house along with Venus. The Sun is posited in the 11th house along with Mars. As Saturn being the *lagna* lord and being in the constellation of the Sun gave the results of the 11th house, i.e. profit. Further in the sub of Jupiter denotes profit through fair means and through services because the Sun is the significator of service and Jupiter denotes kinds of services. Therefore, the native got bank service. The Moon was in the constellation of Jupiter and in the sub of Saturn. Jupiter being the lord of the 12th and 3rd houses denotes journeys and Jupiter aspect on the 9th house shows boost to tate away from the place where native was born. Further the Moon is in sub of Saturn which is also the *lagna* lord and being in its own sign. Sun was in the constellation of Jupiter and in the sub of Mars. Sun is 6th to the 6th (house of service) further strengthening the conclusion. As the Sun was in the sub of Mars which is *swargrahi* in the 11th house shows gains.

2. When the native got married, he was running Saturn *mahadasa*, Rahu *bhukti* and Sun *anterdasa*. Venus was in the constellation of Rahu which is pointed to the 7th house Venus is in the sub of Mercury which is conjoined with Venus in the 10th house. Sun is in the constellation of Jupiter which is aspecting the 7th house and further the Sun is placed in the 7th house in *navamsa*. This clearly shows that the *dasa* and *antardasa* was quite strong to give the results of marriage.

3. The native was blessed with son, in Mercury *mahadasa* Mercury *bhukti* and Mercury *antar*. Mercury was in the constellation of Rahu which is aspected the significator of children. Jupiter, further Rahu is conjoined with Jupiter in *navamsa*. Further the 5th house is aspected by two male planets viz. Mars and Sun therefore the born issue was a male.

Example 2: Born on 18.2.1976 at 6 a.m. at New Delhi
Birth star - Uttarphalguni
Balance of Sun *mahadasa* at birth—1Y 3M 0 D

		Star	**Star lord**	**Sub lord**
Ascendant	= 9s 16°-12'	Shravan	Moon	Sat
Moon	= 5s 7°-6'	Uttarapha-lguni	Sun	Ketu
Jup	= 11s 28°-33'	Revati	Merc	Sat
Sat (R)	= 3s 3°-49'	Puya	Sat	Sat
Mars	= 1s 25°-33'	Mrigshira	Mars	Rahu
Sun	= 10s 4°-56'	Dhanista	Mars	Sun
Ven	= 9s 4°-23'	Uttrasada	Sun	Sat
Merc	= 9s 8°-43'	Uttarasada	Sun	Ven

Rahu	= 6s 24°-25'	Vishaka	Jup	Merc
Ketu	= 0s 24°-25'	Bharani	Ven	Merc

Birth Chart

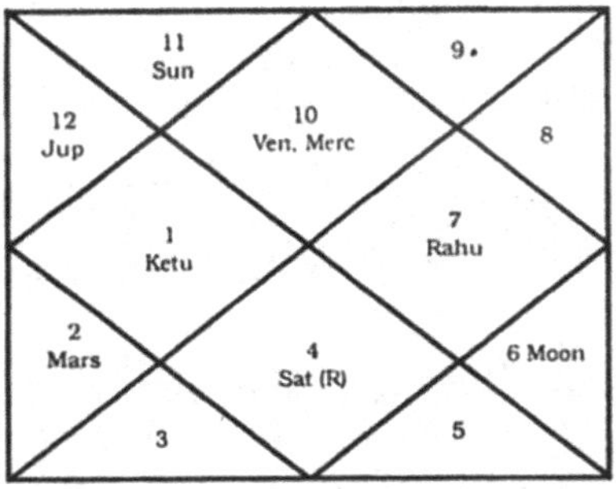

Navamsa

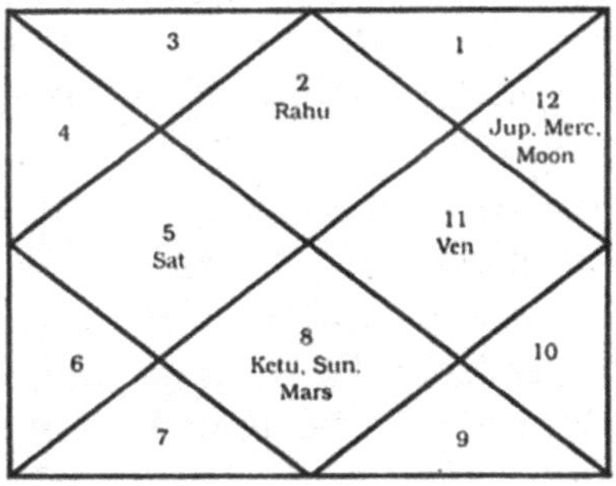

This chart belongs to a young lady. She was adopted when she was an infant. The position of Ketu in the 4th house and the aspect of Saturn on the 4th house and placement of Sat in the 4th *navamsa* clearly shows separation from family. She was reared very affectionately by her adopted parents.

Her adopted father died in Rahu *mahadasa*, Rahu *bhukti* and Ketu *antar*.

Rahu is in the constellation of Jupiter and in the sub of Mercury. Ketu was in the constellation of Venus and in the sub of Mercury. Jupiter is considered to be malefic for Capricorn ascendant and further acted as *Budhksthanapati* lord to the 9th house and placed the 7th and 9th houses. Ketu was in the constellation of Venus which is the 2nd lord to the 9th house. Further Rahu was also second to 9th in natal chart. Therefore, Rahu was to give the results of Jupiter and Ketu was to give the results of Venus. Both gave the results as already said Jupiter was *badhak* to father. Placed 7th to 9th house, Rahu was second to the 9th house, Venus was lord of the 2nd house and 9th house. Both the houses denoting death, ultimately caused of death to her father. Her adopted mother died during Rahu *mahadasa*, Jupiter *bhukti* and Saturn *antar*.

Rahu was in the constellation of Jupiter and in the sub of Mercury. Jupiter was in the constellation of Mercury and in the sub of Saturn. Saturn was in its own constellation and in its own sub.

Rahu was 7th to the 4th house Jupiter was the 12th to the 4th house and malefic aspects of Saturn on the 4th house in inimical sign ended the life of mother. Saturn is also *Badhaksthanpati* lord to the forth house.

She got married during Rahu *mahadasa* Jupiter *bhukti* and Saturn *antar*. Jupiter's aspect on the 7th and 9th houses and placement of Saturn in the 7th house brought here marriage. Jupiter was in the sub of Mercury and Saturn was in its own sub, i.e. Saturn. The sub played very interesting role. Mercury in the lord of the 6th and 9th houses posited in *lagna* with Venus. Mercury and Jupiter boosted her fate but some problems arose and she got entangled in litigation due to the ownership of Mercury of the 6th house. Therefore, Rahu and Jupiter gave her much property but Mercury brought her into court. As Mercury is considered to be an infant among the celestial planets, therefore, the litigation could not be carried on too long. What the sub of Saturn did in her life. Though Saturn is *lagna* lord and placed in the 7th house.

It gave her happiness through marriage but the marriage was unconventional as generally not followed by Hindus because Saturn is malefic by nature.

Example 3: Born on 9.12.1946 at 9.30 p.m. (I.S.T) at 45°N 30' N, 11° 3'E

Birth star — Adra

Balance of Rahu *mahadasa* at birth—11Y 9M 22D

		Constellation	**Constellation Lord**	**Sub lord**
Ascendant	= 3s 28°-30'	Ashelasha	Merc	Sat
Saturn (R)	= 3s 16°-48'	Ashelesha	Merc	Merc
Jupiter	= 6s 24°-31'	Vishaka	Jup	Merc
Venus	= 6S 25°-29'	Vishaka	Jup	Merc
Sun	= 7S 4°-31'	Jyestha	Merc	Rahu
Merc	= 7s 4°-46'	Anuradha	Sat	Sat
Mars	= 8s 2°-37'	Mool	Ketu	Venus
Moon	= 2s 11°-15'	Adra	Rahu	Sat
Rahu	= 1S 19°-39'	Rohini	Moon	Merc
Ketu	= 7S 19°-39'	Jyestha	Merc	Ven

1. This chart belongs to Smt. Sonia Gandhi. When her mother-in-law, Late Smt. Indira Gandhi, was killed; she was running Saturn *mahadasa* and Sun *bhukti*. The 10th house denotes mother-in-law as it in the 4th to the 7th house.

Natal Chart

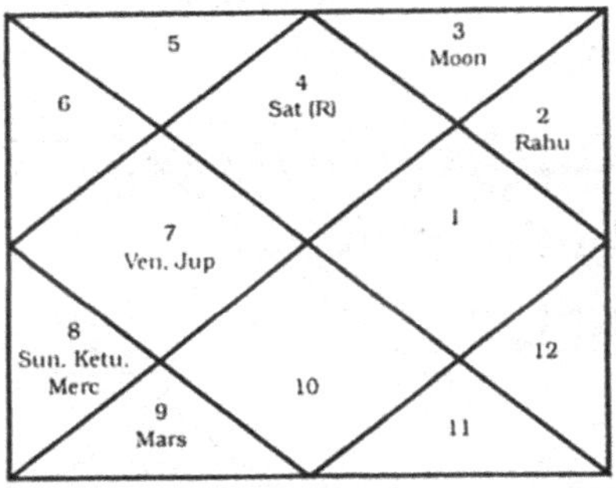

Navamsa

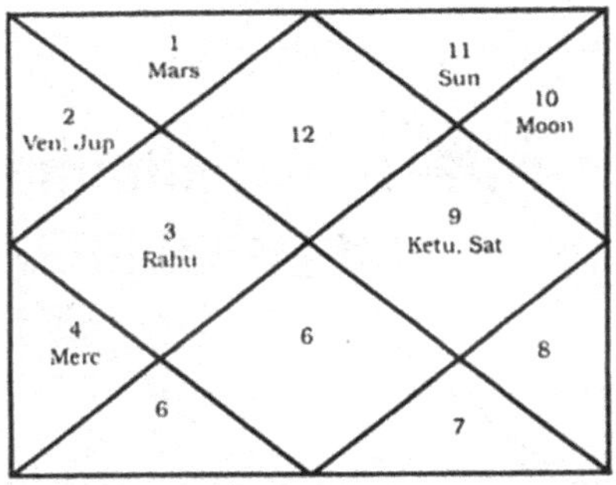

Saturn was *Badhaksthanapati* lord to the 10th house further its debilitated aspect over the 10th house indicated danger to mother-in-law. Saturn was in the constellation of Mercury and in the sub of Mercury. Mercury being the lord of the 12th and 3rd houses placed in the 5th house which is 8th to the 10th house showing danger to the life of mother-in-law. Mercury itself was in the constellation of Saturn. Mercury was also *Badhak* lord to the 10th house in *navamsa* and placed in the fifth house which is 8th to the 10th house. Further Mercury was is *shadasthak* with Saturn in *navamsa*. Thus both Saturn and Mercury became quite malefic strong enough to inflict death on Smt. Indira Gandhi.

2. When her husband Late Rajeev Gandhi was killed, she was under the sway of Saturn *mahadasa* and Jupiter *bhukti*.

Jupiter was in the constellation of Jupiter and in the sub of Mercury which was malefic to her. In *navamsa* Saturn was being aspected by Mars. Thus Mercury became first rate malefic and brought death to her husband.

A RIGHT APPROACH TO DETERMINATION OF PROFESSION (LAWYER'S COMBINATION)

Today in fast changing world, jobs are so varied that it is almost impossible to ascertain the nature of either profession or job with fair degree of accuracy. In ancient times there were limited professions and the criterion of selecting persons for a particular profession or job was also limited. The main occupations or professions of the persons in ancient time were as follows:

1. Agriculture
2. Money lending
3. *Senapati* or Commander in chief
4. *Wazeer* or Prime Minister
5. Business
6. *Dasi* or *Dass*, i.e. lower class of the people who were used to purchase from market to serve affluent class of society including kings.
7. *Vaida* or physician

Therefore, it was possible on the part of the astrologer to predict what profession one will adopt in future, with quite accuracy. Classical texts have given various job assignments to various planets. On that basis it was not difficult to predict the profession or job of the native in ancient times.

In the present scenario while we are at the threshold of 21st century every day new idea is emerging in respect of job or business. In order to keep pace with globalization and to promote business ethics and to meet requisite standards of quality product every organization looks for only those persons who are best suited for the organization. Even in public sector the criteria for selecting a person has drastically changed. This is the situation coupled with mounting unemployment problems not only in India but also in the world as a whole. How can an astrologer predict the deciding nature of job or profession of the person? Is it possible? Yes, it is possible to predict with fair degree of accuracy. But for this the astrologer has to take additional pain in pinpointing the dominating influence of the planet and the concerned house apart form the 10th house. How should then the astrologer proceed to predict about one's mode of job or profession?

It is my humble opinion that astrologers must have a vast knowledge of the subjects which influence the human life. Today every job whether in public sector or private sector requires some sort of eligibility criteria which suit most to the job concerned.

I do not go into the details of every job, however, in a nut-shell, I try to present the basic requirements of the public and private sectors.

1. Education (Today specific education is required for a specific job)
2. Logic
3. Psychology
4. Health
5. Power of arguments
6. Decisive power
7. Planning
8. Execution of planning
9. Behaviour
10. Interaction with the people and so on.

Suppose one person has applied to Indian army. The astrologer has to see, apart health and qualification, that the native must have strong psychology that is required to be an officer of the Indian army and the native is endowed with decisive power. Such considerations are must. We should admit it boldly that job choice dose not rest on the native in India. Increasing unemployment has closed all the doors for candidates. It is only good luck that one gets the job that he dreamed of.

Keeping in view the above statement I discuss the planetary combinations to be a lawyer. While we discuss the cases of lawyers. I present some qualifications to become a successful lawyer:

1. Degree in Law
2. Sharp intellect
3. Correct perception
4. Honesty towards the client
5. Respect for the constitution.

To become a lawyer Saturn, Mars, Jupiter and Rahu must exert their influence on the 10th house in this way that the 6th, 8th and 12th houses gets connected with the 10th house.

In the case of lawyer, houses viz. 8th 6th 12th must exert their influence on the 10th house through Saturn, Mars, Jupiter and Rahu. Saturn and Rahu are termed as malefic and criminal planets though Saturn also makes the native thoughtful and duty conscious. But it is absolutely correct that if Saturn and Rahu are influencing the 6th and 12th houses native comes into contact with disputed persons, criminals or himself gets entangled in various disputes which are settled through either court or at the police station.

Mars makes one daring, energetic and argumentative. Mars in connection with Jupiter either through aspect or conjunction prepares the native to be a good speaker and can thrust his idea or views.

The 10th house is called the house of deeds; one's profession is also ascertained from this house. This house basically deals with the deeds of the native. Deeds are done generally in two ways:

1. When native provides service to other and in lieu of it gets wage or salary and in case of business gets money. When native is in service where he is providing his service to the people and in return gets salary. While in business, he again provides service to the people through products or articles etc and gets money with profit on it.
2. Deeds are done without any gains. Say politics which is said to be a service to the people without any gains. Social reforming, fighting against injustice, etc. are some deeds of the native which are generally done when the native is very sensitive to the miseries of the people and take up the cause of the people as his final mission.

The 10th house produces vibrations which prepare the native to perform his deeds. The 10th house under the dominating influence of planets decides the direction of the deeds of the native. It is also imperative to clear that each house of the horoscope has bearing on other house through their respective lord and each house gets connected with other house through certain relationship. Nine planets and twelve houses of the horoscope have been given various assignments.

The sixth house: It denotes, disputes enmity, etc. which

are settled in court. It is also the 9th house to the 11th house. If the 10th house is the constitution of the nation then the 6th house which is 9th to the 10th denotes justice because the 9th house is said to be *dharma bhava.*

The eighth house: The house of morality of public and code of conduct. Any violation of code of conduct as enumerated by the constitution of India is put up before court. It also shows the income of a lawyer because this is 11th house to the 10th house denoting house of income.

The twelfth house: The house of jail, asylum, hospitals and final liberation. This house not only denotes punishment but also liberation. It is 3rd to the 12th house. The 3rd house is the *prakram bhava.* Thus the 12th house in respect the 10th house becomes *prakram bhava* through which constitution through lawyers passes its orders.

Example 1: Born on 10.07.1891 at 1.18 a.m. (LMT) 13N. 77E35

This example has been taken from Dr. B. V. Raman's book 'How to Judge a Horoscope' vol 2. page 316/317.

Birth Chart

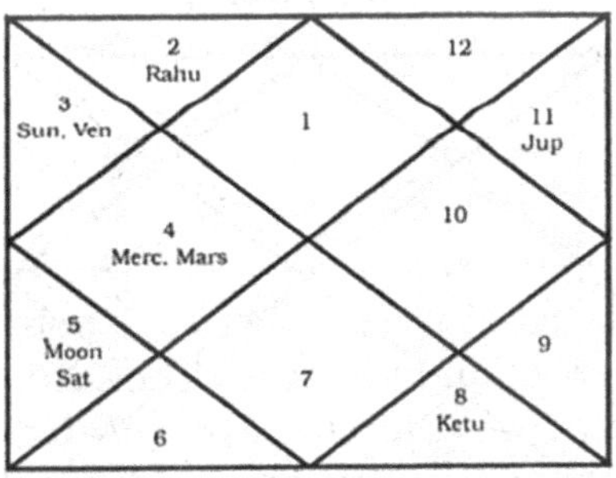

Navamsa

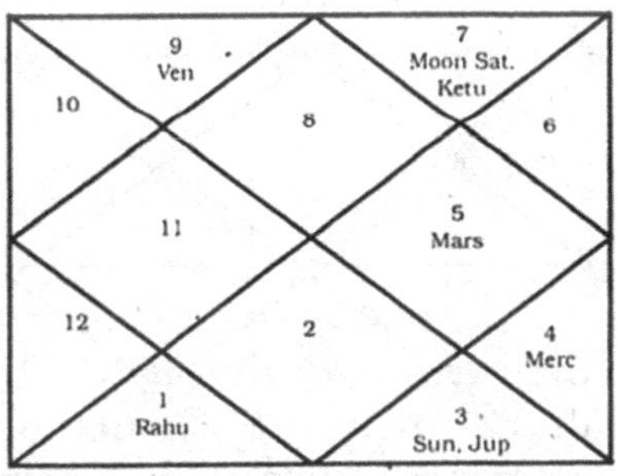

In natal chart the lord of ascendant and the 8th house is placed in the 4th house along with Mercury the lord of the 3rd and 6th houses. Thus houses viz. 6th and 8th get connected with the 10th house.

Similarly, in *navamsa* the lord of the 10th house is placed in the 8th house with Jupiter and lord of the 6th house is placed in the 10th house. Saturn placed in the 12th house aspects Mercury. Jupiter in the 8th aspects Saturn and Moon. Thus the planets viz. Saturn, Jupiter, Mars and Mercury are connected with each other and also houses viz. 6th 8th 10th and

12th. Saturn the lord of the 10th house aspects Jupiter in natal chart. Mercury and Mars also aspect the 10th house. Saturn is said to be a thief or makes the native to earn through unconventional methods. Here mutual aspects between Jupiter and Saturn indicate that Jupiter the planet of *dharma* or justice brings earning through the mediation of Saturn. Further aspect of Mars over the 10th house being the lord of the 8th house and Jupiter denotes that the native is argumentative and a good amount of energy is also utilized for earnings. Secondly, the 8th house's involvement also indicates earnings through unconventional way.

Example 2: Born on 5.11.1870 at 6.49 a.m. (LMT) 22N40, 88E30

(Example taken from 'How to Judge a Horoscope' vol 2, page 316)

Birth Chart

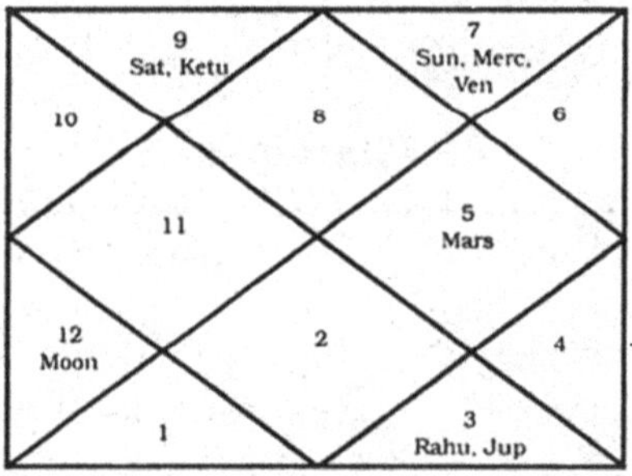

Navamsa

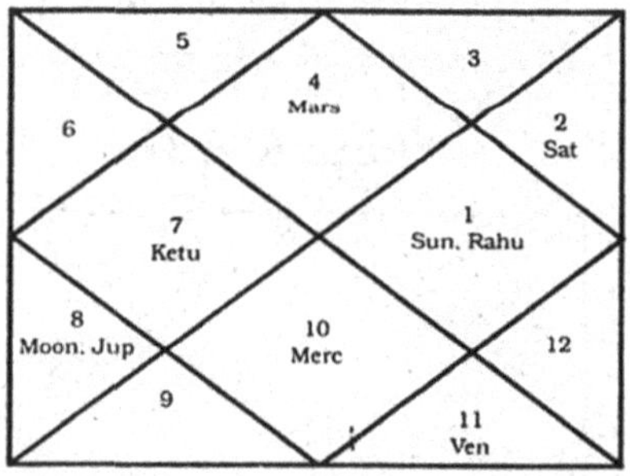

The lord of the 6th house is placed in the 10th house denoting the earning of the native through disputed areas. The lord of the 2nd in the 8th house aspected by Saturn. Thus Saturn, Mars and Jupiter i.e. dispute, crime and justice are involved in respect of the 10th house showing income generation through disputed and unconventional methods and involvement of Jupiter clearly indicates the dispensation of justice to the people.

The native could not stick to his profession because the lord of the 10th house both in natal chart and *navamsa* is debilitated clearly showing *vichheda* (separation from profession). In navamsa the 8th house is aspected by two unconventional planets, i.e. Saturn and Mars. The mutual aspect between Jupiter and Saturn creates a natural urge for justice and native detaches himself from foul play with the clients.

Example 3: Born on 10.11.1934 at 8.28 p.m. at Allahabad.

The native was a lawyer of high court Allahabad, had good rise in his profession as a lawyer. Presently, he is at the zenith of his career in politics. Argumentative, sober, well learned and possess remarkable decisive power.

Birth Chart

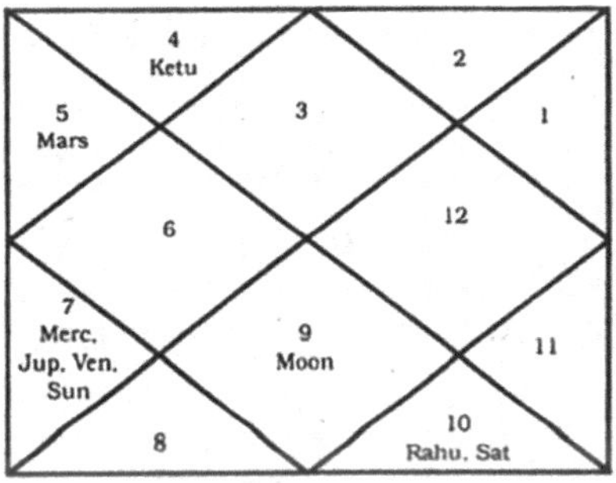

Navamsa

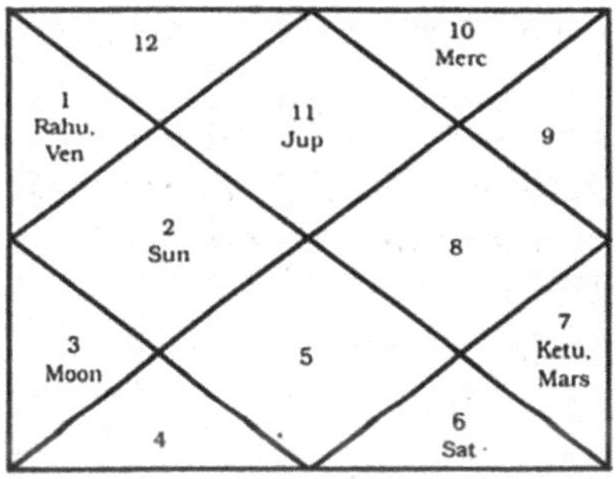

The ascendant of the native falls in Rahu star Arudha. Mercury, the lord of ascendant, is also in Rahu star Swati. Mercury, the planet of intellect being in Rahu star, clearly denotes the association of the native with disputes. As Rahu is conjunct with Saturn (the planet of discuputes) clearly denotes the association of the native with disputed persons.

Saturn the lord of the 8th and 9th houses aspects the 10th house. Mars the lord of the 6th and 11th houses aspects the 10th house. Thus two malefics aspect the 10th house. Saturn aspects Jupiter, Mercury, Venus and Sun. Therefore, Jupiter, the lord of the 10th house, was under the influence of Saturn which is placed in the 8th house which happens to be the 11th house to the 10th house. Therefore, Mars, Saturn, Jupiter and Rahu all are involved in shaping his profession.

In *navamsa* too the lord of the 10th house, i.e. Mars is placed in the 9th house. The 10th house is aspectd by Saturn, Jupiter aspects Mars thus tones down the vicious nature of Mars and allows him to generate only positive vibrations.

Example 4: Born on 20.04.1955 at 7.30 p.m. at Agra.

The native is a well known lawyer of Agra. Nice and sober man well educated and takes part in political activities too.

The ascendant falls in Swati star of Rahu and aspected by Saturn. Saturn also aspects the 10th house. The lord of the 10th house is placed in the 6th house with exalted Venus who

Birth Chart

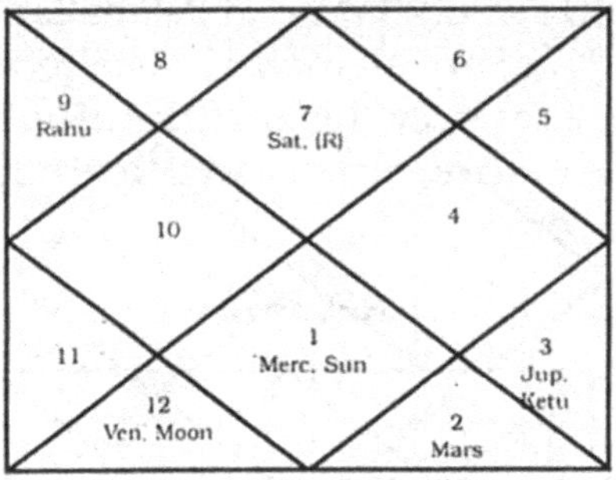

Navamsa

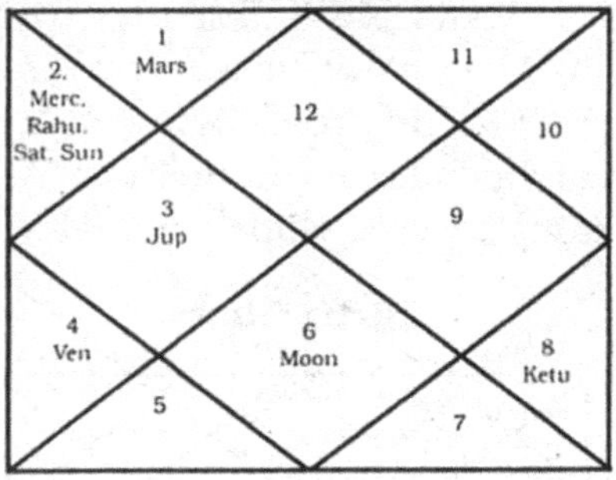

happens to be the lord of the 8th house. Both Venus and Moon aspect the 12th house. Thus the 10th house has both malefic and benefic influences. Venus and Moon in the 6th house, which happens to be the 9th to the 10th house, clearly shows his sincerity in his profession. Saturn's aspect on the 10th house shows earnings through unconventional methods. It is absolutely correct in his case as he is an advocate but so far he has not taken any false case, he is sincere and truthful to his clients.

Example 5: Born on 16.11.1966 at 8.17 p.m. at New Delhi.

The native is a lawyer of Tees Hazari Court, Delhi. He is pleasant, charming and argumentative.

The lord of the 10th house, i.e. Jupiter aspects the 8th house. Mars the lord of the 6th house aspects Saturn and 10th house. Thus the 6th and 8th houses influence the 10th house through there lord viz. Mars, Saturn and Jupiter.

Birth Chart

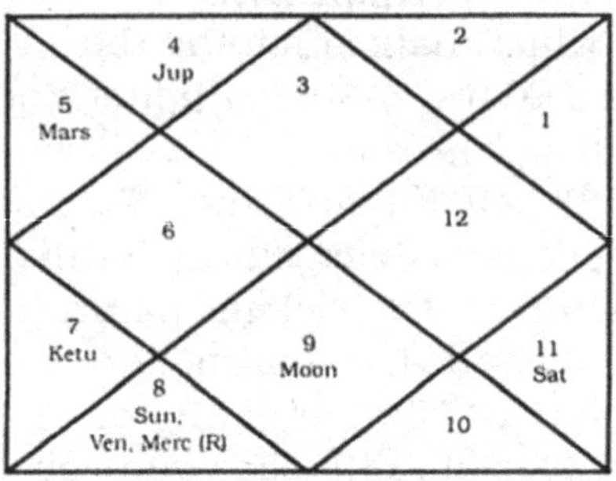

Navamsa

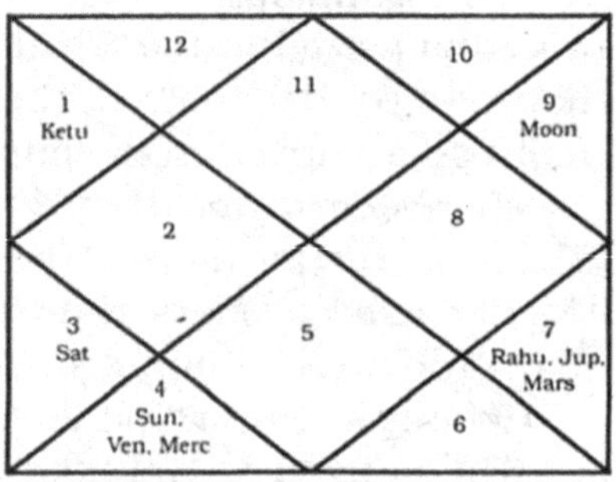

After discussing the above cases, the entire theory can be summarized as follows;

1. Ascendant should have a connection with Saturn or

Rahu because these two planets associate the native with disputes, thieves, and criminals.

2. Ascendant, either in fierce sign or intellectual sign makes the native argumentative and intellectual sign makes him thoughtful.

3. The 6th and 8th houses at least must have a connection with the 10th house because the 6th house denotes disputes and the 8th house shows unconventional methods.

4. Saturn and Mars if influencing the 10th house must be inspected either by Mercury, Venus or Jupiter. If Jupiter or Venus or Mercury placed in either 6th or 8th house denotes that the native is sincere in his dealings.

HORARY ASTROLOGY—THE SUBLIME ART OF PREDICTION

Horary astrology is the branch of astrology which deals with the moment of query. A few well known astrologers of India even preferred horary astrology to natal astrology. The reasons of preferring horary to natal astrology were explained by them with scientific reasons:

1. Horary astrology depends on the present time, there is no error of time. While in natal astrology the error of time may be present.
2. Horary astrology is related with the mind of querist and reflects his true position the nature and the contents of the questions.
3. Horary astrology deals with the transit position of the planet of the moment and immediately puts up the planetary positions of the moments before the astrologer.

'Horary Astrology' by Neelkantha and the 'Prashana Marga' by Dr. B. V. Raman deals with the subject exhaustively. The work of late Dr. Raman was based on traditional astrology and had given very useful tips on the subjects. Here I would like to mention the name of late Prof. K. S. Krishnamurty, who was considered as the master of horary astrology and developed this method of prediction to its near perfection.

This article blends the methods of Late K.S. Krishnamurty and the traditional horary astrology and endeavours to put before esteemed readers the logic and reason behind the new method.

General Outlines of the Method of Late K.S. Krishnamurty

Constellation Division: Late Krishnamurty divided 27 constellations of the zodiac into 249 and included the theory of sub lord in the method. Sub lord is nothing new but the smallest division of the *nakshatra.* According to Krishnamurty constellation decides about the matter to whom or which it refers while the sub lord decides the nature of the result whether good or bad, success or failure.

Moon: The Moon is the significator of mind and deserves special mention in the books of Late Krishnamurty because the query asked by the querist must relate with the position, and occupation of the constellation by the Moon and the lord of the constellation. If the query is related with the Moon then the intention of the querist is honest.

Ruling Planets: According to late Krishnamurty there are five ruling planets.

1. Ascendant lord
2. Ascendant star lord
3. Moon sign lord
4. Moon star lord
5. Day lord

Day lord is the lord in usual manner. For example, Sunday is ruled by the Sun, while Monday is rules by the Moon and so on. The importance of ruling planets is in timing.

House Division: Hindu system of astrology considers each house of the zodiac to be of 30 degrees. Therefore, as per Hindu system of astrology each house extends up to 30 degrees and always constant, i.e. fix zodiac. Late Krishnamurty divided the houses of a zodiac. In this method one house may extend upto 35 degrees or may be 27 degrees but the total of the twelfth house never exceeds 360 degrees. He used the word cusp, the exact point where the house begins. Therefore, his house division was called **cuspal division** or **cuspal charts**.

General Theory of Krishnamurty

1. According to Krishnamurty, there is no specific role of signs (*rasis*) constellation of the planets. However, retrogression is related with negation etc. his method takes into account the importance of constellations (in Vedas constellations are mentioned, not *rasis. Rasis* were discovered in the latter part). He says that planet posited in the constellation gives the result of the lord of the constellation. If the Sun is placed in Kritika star then during its *mahadasa* the Sun will give the result of Ketu and so on.

2. He divided a constellation into 249 parts and asked the querist to give only one number. Here the emphasis is put on the number given by the querist.

How Osho Astrological Research Centre Deals with Horary Astrology

1. According to the method of K. S. Krishnamurty number is asked from the querist. Querist is advised that he must give the number only when he has natural strong urge to know the matter.

2. The birth chart is erected of the time of query using either Lahiri's *ayanamsa* or Krishnamurty's *aynamsa* with the latitude and longitude of the place from where query is to be answered.

3. *Prastharashtak charka* is also worked out to know the transit position of the planet of the moment.

4. As per traditional method of horary astrology, Jupiter is specifically judged. According to the director of the centre Padamshree Gopal Das Neeraj ji, if Jupiter as per traditional method aspects ascendant, the querist will realize his desire.

5. Osho Astrological Research Centre, Agra has prepared 249 house division tables as ready reckoner using Raphel's table of house division at 27 degrees 11 minutes for Agra and Krishnamurty's *aynamsa*.

Let us discuss a few cases which would be helpful in understanding these methods clearly.

Example 1: On dated 14.2.99 at 2.40 p.m. at Agra a lady, turned about 38 years, asked about her marriage in future. She also told that she was divorced by his husband. She gave me number 49.

As per **Krishnamurty method**

(Horoscope and other details on page-11)

Cusps	**Sign**	**Star lord**	**Sub lord**
1st Cusp=2s 10d-26m	Merc	Rahu	Sat
2nd Cusp=3s 3d-15m	Moon	Jup	Rahu
3rd Csup=3s 28d-15m	Moon	Merc	Sat
4th Cusp=4s 27d-15m	Sun	Sun	Sun
5th Cusp=6s 1d-15m	Ven	Mars	Merc
6th Cusp=7s 7d 15m	Mars	Sat	Merc
7th Cusp=8s 10d-26m	Jup	Ketu	Sat
8th Cusp=9s 13d-15m	Sat	Sun	Sat
9th Cusp=9s 28d-15m	Sat	Mars	Sat
10th Cusp=10s 27d-15m	Sat	Jup	Ven

11th Cusp=0s 1d-15m	Mars	Ketu	Ven
12th Cusp=1s 7d-15m	Ven	Sun	Ketu

For the second marriage 2nd, 11th and 7th houses are to be judged:

Cuspal Chart

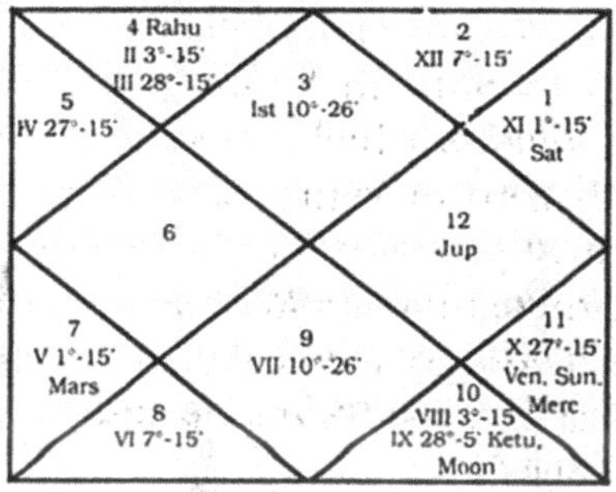

7th Cusp=8s 10d-26m	Jup	Ketu	Sat
2nd Cusp=3s 3d-15m	Moon	Jup	Rahu
11th Cusp=0s 1d-15m	Mars	Ketu	Ven

According to first the 7th cusp sub lord, i.e. Saturn which is placed in the 11th house in Aries sign. Saturn is placed in constellation of Ketu and in the sub of Mars. Therefore, above condition is not fulfilled.

The sub lord of the 7th cusp, i.e. Saturn though placed in the 11th house becomes significator, yet Saturn being in debilitation and in the star of Ketu which in no way influences any of the house mentioned above.

Therefore, she was told not to have any hope for second marriage.

As per **Tadiotional Method**

The horoscope worked out on dated 14.2.99 at 2.40 p.m. at Agra

The lord of the 7th house is placed in the 10th house in his own sign. The 7th house is not aspected by any of the planet. Since Jupiter is beset with *kendrathpati dasa* does not indicateairly well chances. The *dasa* at the time of query was Sun *mahadasa* and Venus *antaredasa*. Venus being the natural significator of marriage gives hope for marriage, however, it is second marriage, therefore, the 8th house must also be connected. The lord of the 8th house is debilitated, therefore, weakening the prospects of marriage. Bhttopla in 'Prasana Gyana' says that if the moon is aspected by Jupiter one can have marriage partner but if malefics aspect such Moon then prospects of marriage are remote. In the chart Moon is not aspected by Jupiter and Mars aspects over Moon. therefore, prospects seem to be remote.

Prastharashtak Varga: The *dasa* lord Sun gives only two *bindus* in his own *prastarashtak chakra* while *Bhukti nath*, i.e. Venus gives zero to Sun. In Venus *prastarak chakra* though Venus gives five *bindus* which is considered just an average yet the Sun gives zero to Venus. Therefore. *prastarak chakra* too does not indicate ambition to be realized. It is interesting to note that in *sarvasthak chakra* the 2nd and 11th houses get only 15 and 26 *bindus* respectively. According to the general rule of Asthakvarga at least 28 *bindus* must be in the concerned house to get it flourish.

Consclusion: Thus above study reveals absolute denial of marriage. She is unmarried till date.

Example 2: One of the very influential persons of India gave me the number 131 on telephone and wanted to know about his foreign trips and litigations which were pending in various courts of India.

Krishnamurty Padhati:

Overseas Queston

(1) If the sub lord of the 11th cusp, in any way, connected with the 9th and 11th houses or with their lords one goes to overseas.

(2) No. 131 denotes Libra ascendant. The 12 cusp were worked out using Raphael's table of houses.

Cusp	Sign	Star lord	Sub lord
1st Cusp-6s 8d-40m	Ven	Rahu	Jup
2nd Cusp-7s 7d-33m	Mars	Sat	Ketu
3rd Cusp-8s 8d-33m	Jup	Ketu	Jup
4th Cusp-9s 10d-33m	Sat	Moon	Moon
5th Cusp=10s 12d-33m	Sat	Rahu	Sat
6th Cusp=11s 8d-33m	Jup	Sat	Ven
7th Cusp=0s 8d-40m	Mars	Ketu	Jup
8th Cusp=1s 7d-33m	Ven	Sun	Ketu
9th Cusp=2s 8d-33m	Merc	Rahu	Rahu
10th Cusp=3s 10d-33m	Moon	Sat	Sun

11th Cusp=4s12d-33m	Sun	Ketu	Merc
12th Cusp=5s12d-33m	Merc	Moon	Rahu

Cuspal Chart

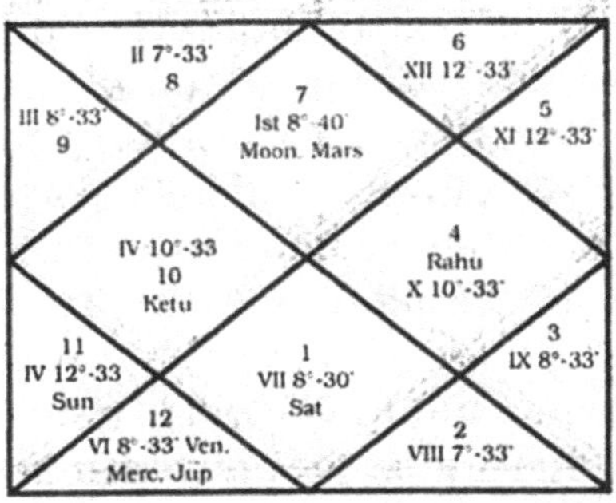

(i) The sub lord of the 11th cusp, i.e. Mercury happens to be the lord of the 9th and 12th houses and placed with the lord of the 3rd cusp, i.e. Jupiter and aspects the 12th house. Therefore, oversea journey is promised. But when?

(ii) At the time of query Jupiter *mahadasa* and Saturn *antardasa* was operating which lasts up to 10.06.2001

(iii) The ruling planets are as follows:

Ascendant lord —Venus
Ascendant star lord—Rahu
Moon sign lord —Venus
Moon star lord—Jupiter
Day lord—Sun

He was predicted to go to foreign during Jupiter *mahadasa* and Saturn *antardasa* after 23.11.99. Because Venus is one of the ruling planets and deposited in the constellation of Mercury.

Litigations: Since litigation is the matter of the 6th and 10th houses. The 10th house denotes government and the court is representative of the Indian constitution. The sub lord of the 6th cusp happens to be connected with the 11th cusp or the lord of 11th house then one is exonerated from the charges.

The sub lord of 6th cusp, i.e. Venus was placed in the 6th house and aspects the 12th house, therefore, ruling out the possibility of his going to the court. Secondly, the lord of the 11th cusp, i.e. the Sun is placed in the Sun of Jupiter which aspects the 10th house. Therefore, two benefics aspect over the 12th and 10th houses and promise his exoneration from all charges. It will also happen after 24.11.1999.

Traditional Method: The horoscope was erected on dated 7.3.99 at 6.40 p.m.

The ascendant falls in Leo sign and the Sun was placed in the 7th house. The house connected with foreign relations Jupiter was aspecting 12th house and Mercury the lord of the 11th house was also aspecting the 12th house. The lord of the 9th house was placed in the 3rd house along with the *karaka of jala* (water) in the 3rd house and aspection its own sign. Thus all the houses of travelling viz. 9th 12th and 3rd were well connected.

Prastharastak Chakra: On dated 7th March 99, the *mahadasa* lord Jupiter gave four *bindus* to his own *prastaraka* and the *Bhukti nath* Saturn too give *bindu* to Jupiter while Saturn was benefic of any *bindu* in its *prastarak*, therefore, he was told that after denials and dejection, he would be able to go overseas.

Conclusions: After verifiying the method he was declared that in January 2000 he would go over seas. As per Krishnamurty Padhati the date was declared after 23.11.1999. *Prastakrak Chakra* helped in delineating transit results and reacting at one point.

Example 3: One person gave me number 11 on telephone from Bhopal and wanted to know when he would be reinstated?

(Horscope and other details on page 16.)

The question was taken up on dated 29.05.1999 at 6.43 a.m. at Agra.

Krishnamurty Padhati

1. **Reinstatement in Service**: The houses 2nd, 6th, and 10th were judged. Since the second house denotes income, the 6th house is the house of service and the 10th house denotes employer. If the sub lord of the 10th cusp is in the constellation whose ruler if becomes significator of either 6th or 2nd or 10th house, one is reinstated.

2. No. 11 denotes Aries ascendant. The 12th cusp was worked out using Raphael's table of house division.

Cusp	Sign	Star lord	Sub lord
1st Cusp=0s 15d-33m	Mars	Ven	Sun
2nd Cusp=1s 15d-25m	Ven	Moon	Jup
3rd Cusp=2s 9d-25m	Merc	Rahu	Jup
4th Cusp=3s 3d-25m	Moon	Sat	Sat
5th Cusp=4s 0d-25m	Sun	Ketu	Ketu
6th Cusp=5s 5d-25m	Merc	Sun	Merc
7th Cusp=6s 15d-33m	Ven	Rahu	Ven
8th Cusp=7s 15d-25m	Mars	Sat	Jup
9th Cusp=8s-29d-25m	Jup	Ketu	Sat
10th Cusp=9s 3d-25m	Sat	Sun	Sat
11th Cusp=10s 0d-25m	Sat	Mars	Merc
12th Cusp=11s 5d-25m	Jup	Sat	Sat

Cuspal Chart

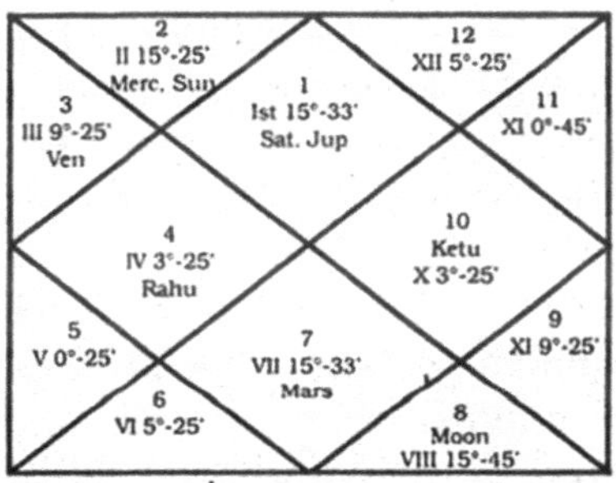

1. The sub lord of the 10th cusp, i.e. Saturn is placed in the star of Venus which happens to be the lord of the 2nd house and is placed in the 3rd house which happens to be 2nd to the 2nd house. Secondly, the sub lord of the 11th cusp, i.e. Mercury is placed in the 2nd house being the lord of the 6th house. Therefore, these pieces of information are ample to declare boldly that he will be reinstated. The next question is— when.

2. Ruling planets are as follows:

Ascendant lord—Mars (R)
Ascendant star lord ——Venus
Moon sign lord——Mars
Moon star lord—Jupiter
Day lord——Saturn

Mahadasa of Jupiter and the Moon *bhukti* operates up to 19 Jan 2000. He was told that after mid September 1999 he would be reinstated when he would be under the sway of Jup/ Moon/Sat. Jupiter is in the star of Ketu, which is placed in the 10th house in the sign Saturn. Saturn is in the star of Venus which is significator of the 2nd house and the Moon is in the state of Jupiter and Ketu happens to be in the star of Moon, therefore, their conjoined period must give him service and the conjoined period would be operating from mid September 1999.

Traditional Method: Since in Gemini ascendant Venus is considered to be the most benefic planet and she is placed in ascendant and exchanges sign with lord of Mercury. The *dasa nath* Jupiter being the lord of the 10th house is placed in the 11th house. In *navamsa* Jupiter aspects ascendant and the lord of ascendant placed in the 9th house. The only factor is that the entry into the service is not smooth and involves litigation and delay because debilitated Moon is placed in the 6th house the house of service and the lord of the 6th house is in the 5th house which happens to be 12th to the 6th house.

Prastarasthak Chakra: Jupiter has given 4 *bindus* in his own *prastarasthak varga*. Moon gives 6 *bindus* in her *prastarasthak varga*. Saturn has contributed 4 *bindus* in its *prastarasthak* and specially given one *bindu* to Venus since Saturn has transited Bharani star, therefore, it has to give the results of Venus. And in both the methods Venus becomes strong significator of service. *Prastarasthak* also assures reinstatement in the service. [Horoscope on page-17]

Example 4: One person gave me number 28 and he wanted to know about his promotion.

The question was taken up for judgement on dated 4 feb 1999 at 9.13 p. m. at Agra.

Krisnamurthi Padhati: 1. For promotions houses viz. 2nd, 6th, 10th and 11th are to be judged. If the sub lord of the eleventh cusp is the significator of either 2 or 10 and in any way connected with the 6th house, native's desire is fulfilled.

2. Number 28 denotes Taurus ascendant and subsequently other cusps were also worked out using Krishnamurty's *Aynamsa* and Raphael's table of house division.

Cuspal Chart

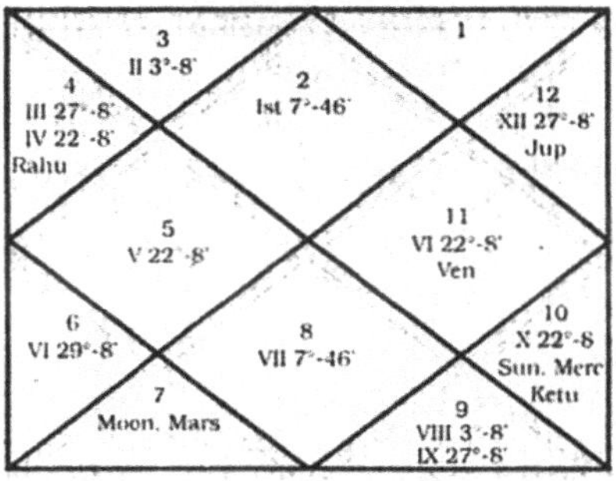

Cusp	Sign	Star lord	Sub lord
1st Cusp=1s 7d-46m	Venus	Sun	Venus
2nd Cusp=2s 3d-8m	Merc	Mars	Venus
3rd Cusp=2s 27d-8m	Merc	Jup	Venus
4th Cusp=3s 22d-8m	Moon	Merc	Sun
5th Cusp=4s 22d-8m	Sun	Venus	Sat
6th Cusp=5s 29d-8m	Merc	Mars	Sat
7th Cusp=7s 7d-46m	Mars	Sat	Ketu
8th Cusp= 8s 3d-8m	Jup	Ketu	Sun
9th Cusp=8s 27d-3m	Jup	Sun	Sun
10th Cusp=9s 22d-8m	Sat	Moon	Ven
11th Cusp=10s 22d-8m	Sat	Jup	Sat
12th Cusp=11s 29d-8m	Jup	Merc	Sat

3. The sub lord of the 11th cusp, i.e. Saturn is also the sub lord of the 6th cusp and aspects the 6th house and happens to be the lord of the 10th house. In this way one sub lord becomes the significator of all the houses concerned. The sub lord of the 10th cusp, i.e. Venus happens to be the sub lord of the 2nd cusp and placed in the 10th house being the lord of the 6th house. Therefore, again promotion is assured. But when?

4. **Ruling Planets** were as follows:

Ascendant lord—Venus
Ascendant star lord—Sun
Moon sign lord ——Venus
Moon star lord——Sun
Day lord——Jupiter

The querist was told that he would be promoted and transferred after mid May 1999.

Reason: Since Saturn the lord of the 10th and 11th houses, was placed in the 12th house. The 12th house denotes separation and distant place. The querist was promoted in Sun/Venus/ Saturn period in mid May 99 and was transferred to Gwalior.

Traditional Method

As per traditional method Virgo was rising in the east on dated 4.2.1999 at 9.13 p.m. at Agra. Jupiter was aspecting ascendant itself was the clear testimony that his desire would be realized. Further Jupiter, Mercury, Sun all were aspecting 11th house, the house of profit. Since the Sun, lord of the 12th house, was conjoined with Mercury, therefore,. transfer was indicated with profit. Secondly, the lord of the 2nd house, i.e. Venus was placed in friendly sign in the 6th house, i.e. the house of service and was aspecting the 12th house. Such indications were clear the testimony in proving above prediction.

Prastarasthak Varga: At the moment of query the *dasanath* i.e. Sun gave 5 *bindus* in its own *Prastarasthak varga*. The *Bhuktinath*, i.e. Venus gave one *bindu* to Sun in *Prastarasthak varga*. Venus also gave one *bindu* in her own *Prastarasthak varga*. Therefore, *Prastarasthak varga* also ensured the success of predictions.

A NEW APPROACH TO MATCHING OF CHARTS

Matching of charts before marriage is customary in India. It has been given an important place which can be judged from the fact that in the absence of horoscopes, the matching is done with the help of NAME RASI (NAAM RASI). What is the logic behind matching the horoscopes with NAAM RASI is not clear to me. Neither I am able to understand the scientific reason of it. But such matching of charts is frequently undertaken by astrologers. The Classical texts have simplified the procedure and restricted the matching of charts to maximum 36 times or minimum 18 times comparison of VASYA, VARNA, NADI, etc. of the would be bride and bridegroom. Even in the list of traditional way of matching a few points have been emphasized viz. Nadi and *Mangal Dosa.* It has not been scientifically explained by the astrologers what is meant by *Nadi dosa* and what is role of Mangal in married life? If Mangal or Mars is considered to be malefic then Saturn should also be considered from this point of view, because Saturn is also the first rate malefic and a new conception of *Sani Dosa* though the role of Saturn is delaying the marriage is quite evident.

The entire foundation of future rests on married life, because marriage in India does not only provide conjugal happiness but also paves the way for future generations and future generations through their nature, temperament, behaviour shape the society and the whole structure of the world through their more or less contribution. It is said that marriages are made in heaven. As marriages are made in heaven where does the divorce take place? There is no fault in the system of God. Follies, weakness, brutalities, etc. are a part of human beings. So matching of chart from marriage point of view must be taken as a mission. It is the duty of an astrologer that he must present the entire picture before the parents. It is better for the beginners and the astrologers, who do not posses deep knowledge of the subject to avoid matching of horoscopes and must say boldly let it be matched by the competent astrologers.

Keeping in view the time ahead it can be said that the traditional way of matching is not competent enough and requires improvement on the part of open minded and research oriented scholars of astrology. I would like to discuss the role of a few planets and their conjunction with other planets which are directly related with the married life.

Mars-Venus: It is the most unfortunate conjunction as far as married life is concerned. Some astrologers have branded this conjunction as a clear cut signal of debauchery. In narrow sense it is correct, but in broader sense keeping in view the innate qualities and psychology of human beings it is not correct.

If this combination persists in the horoscope of a person who is a layman, his chances of extra marital relations are more pronounced and the person is only sex hungry. If this combination is found in the horoscope of a learned person or person with some outstanding abilities, the combination directs his energy from outer world to inner world of consciousness. His appetite for sex is transformed towards his goal. The lust for body is transformed into the lust for destination. This combination conceals with in its orbits both venom and nectar as Rahu possesses both venom and nectar. In case of an ordinary person where this combination exists becomes sex hunter not the reason being fed up with spouse but not getting mental satisfaction. Just in the quest of mental satisfaction, they change partners. If readers remember the statement of Mr. Bill Clinton when got entangled in Monica Lewinsky episode he said in one of the interviews that he needed sex when he felt alone and wanted mental peace. This combination is present in the horoscope of Mr. Bill Clinton. Had he been only sex hunter, he would not have touched such a great height. It is also true that this combination makes one intelligent and learned. If this combination is found in the 7th house (the house denotes marriage in very narrow sense but in broader sense it is the house showing the flow of energy towards the construction of outer world) and other favourable factors are present then one becomes the seeker of one's inner consciousness as happened in the case of late Dr. B. V. Raman.

Venus-Mercury: This combination too have been considered to be an unscrupulous as far as married life is concerned. According to some astrologers this combination makes the native to be oversexed. In a number of horoscopes examined by me produced just contrary results and these results were told me by the natives themselves. This combination rather making them oversexed depressed their sexual life and diverted their attention to fine beauty of artistic pursuit of life. The reason for depressed sex is simple. Mercury is considered to be eunuch planet and its association with Venus, the planet of sex, Mars the sexual capacity of Venus.

Mangal Dosa: This is much hyped and the most controversial aspect of horoscopes. The placement of Mars in the 1st, 2nd, 4th, 7th, 8th and 12th houses is considered the horoscope to be with *Mangal Dosa*. It has not been clear so far why *Mangal Dosa* is so dreaded and why so much fuss is created about this *dosa*? The explanation to this *dosa* has been given as the killer of either wife or husband. No other clarification has been given so far.

The learned editor of this magazine at one point comments that Mars denoting husband in female nativity is scientifically and philosophically correct.

Mars is the planet criminal and malefic effects, its association with any planet .erodes the quality of the planet and brings about a substantial change in the behaviour of the planet. The association of Mars with Moon causes *Sasi-Mangal* or *Chandra Mangal Yoga*. This *yoga* coincides with wealth and luxury of life.

This is also a case of *Mangal Dosa* and this *yoga* makes the native to run behind the money and can go to any extent in pursuit of money, simultaneously it erodes relations with mother. *Kunj Dosa* is judged from ascendant, Moon and Venus. Here I deviate slightly from various traditional schools of thoughts because of concentrating on the main theme for this paper. As far as *Kunj Dosa* is to be judged in respect of marriage, it should be judged from Venus and the lord of the 7th house. The association of Mars either with Venus or the 7th lord creates unusal sexual lust. As said earlier this association has both venom and nectar. However, Mars *dosa* gets nullified if it is aspected by Jupiter. The aspect of Jupiter over Mars-Venus conjunction leads to high class spirituality provided Saturn is beneficially placed. It is also to be worth mentioning that Kunj *dosa* is specially to be judged in the horoscopes of females. The placement of Mars in either ascendant or in the 7th house is to be specially judged. At these two positions Mars generally gives rise to short and hot tempered one and lustful wife respectively.

The role of the Sun, Rahu and Saturn has not been discussed because the effect in general is known to readers and astrologers. The placement of Mars in the 1st, 2nd, 4th, 7th, 8th and 12th houses as enunciated by classical texts to be the case of Mangal *dosa* has direct bearings on the qualities of the concerned houses. But in the said position, except ascendant and the 7th house, Mangal *dosa* is not related with married life specifically.

The spouse should also be *mangali* to encounter the evil effect of this *dosa*. The hypothesis could be considered only on the ground that for *mangali kanya*, who have excessive sexual power must have husband with equal sexual power atleast above average. It is also imperative in the context to discuss whether placement is powerful or aspect. Late K. S. Krishnamurthy strongly recommended that tenant is stronger, i.e. placement is more powerful. This statement is correct in this case of Sun, Moon, Mercury and Venus. But in the case of Jupiter, Saturn and Mars aspect should be given equal importance. In majority of cases it has been noticed that the aspects of Jupiter, Saturn and Mars are powerful than their placement. This statement can be verified from the very fact that these three planets have been given additional aspect-power.

In case of Mars, it aspects either ascendant or the 7th house or Venus or the 7th lord it clearly indicates some sort of bickerings in the married life.

The above theory must be specially judged in Taurus, Cancer, Scorpio and Capricorn ascendant because in Taurus ascendant the 7th house happens to be Scorpio. The ascendant the 7th house falls in Capricorn and Mars acts as *badhaksthanapati* lord to Capricorn. In case of *Katak* ascendant the *badhakshtana* for the 7th house is the 5th house, the house of children. In Scorpio ascendant the 7th house happens to be Taurus, the natural enemy sign of Mars.

In case of Capricorn ascendant where 7th house happens to be *Katak* where Mars is said to be in debilitated stage and further Mars is *badhak* lord being the lord of the 11th house which happens to be the 5th to the 7th house. Therefore, Mangal *dosa* is to be judged logically rather than traditionally.

Let us examine some charts in the light of above statement. Here I discuss two charts supplied to me by the concerned parents from the point of view of marriage.

Boy: DOB 20.05.1974 born at Agra 11:20 p.m.

Girl: DOB 01.01.1975 born at Moradabad (U.P.) at 3.39 a.m.

Natal Chart of Boy

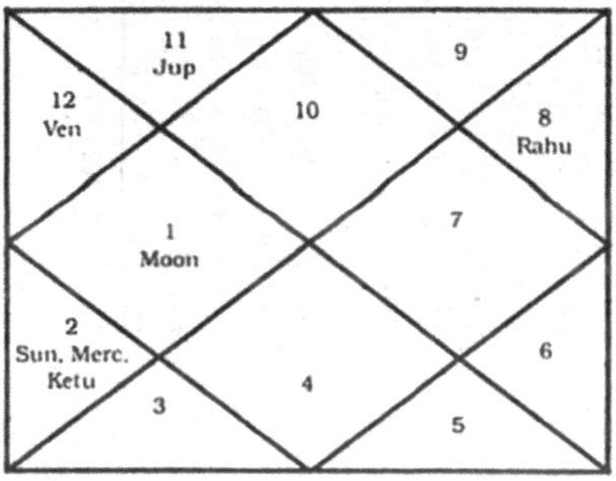

Natal Chart of Girl

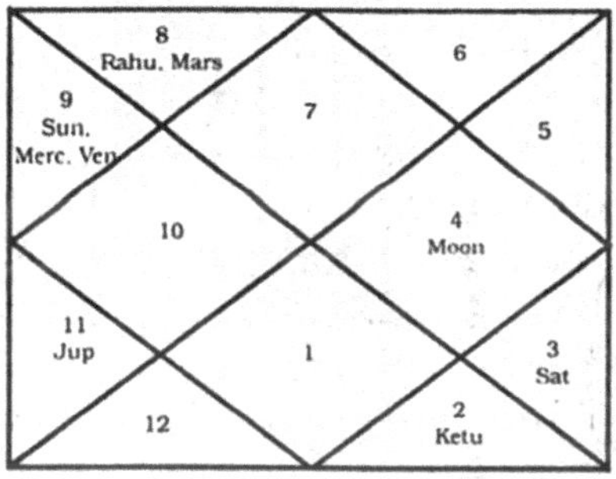

MATCHING OF CHARTS

	Boy	Girl	Points	Reason
(1)	The ascendant falls in Capricorn sign ruled by Saturn. The *rajyogk-arka* for this asd is Venus.	The ascendant falls in Libra sign ruled by Venus. The *raj-yogkarka* for this ascendant is Saturn	6	The ascendant is considered to be the basic foundation of life on which depends the qualities, temperament and other habits. In that case both Venus and Saturn exert their predominating role. Venus and Saturn are bosson friends and the ascendants concerned are friendly to each other.
(2)	The 7th house is ruled by Moon and she is placed In Aries sign.	The 7th house is ruled by Mars and Moon is placed in her own sign i.e. Cancer.	- 6	In that case 7th house denotes same qualities. As in case of boy Moon is placed in Aries sign where she derives some sort of vibrations of Mars. In case of girl her 7th house falls in Aries sign and further Moon is placed in Karka which happens to be the 7th house of boy. Thus the vibrations connected with the 7th house have equal bearings.
(3)	The natural significator of marriage. i.e. Venus is exalted which happens to be *rajyogkaraka* for Capricorn ascendant.	Venus is placed along with Sun and Mercury and aspected by Saturn.	4	In case of boy the Venus is unafflicted and has given rise to fondness for luxurious life and imagination for artisitic pursuit of life. In case of girl Venus is afflicted by Sun and the Saturn. Here the Venusians qualities are

				depressed. However. Lagnesh and the Sun in 3rd house provide her impetus to make her own image. Saturn the rajyogkaraka turns Venus to express her self in art. She is good vocal singer. Thus both the boy and girl have likings for artistic life. However afflicted Venus of girl is a problem.
(4)	The 7th house from Moon falls in Libra sign.	The 7th house from Moon falls in Capricorn sign.	6	As discussed above both are friendly to each other.
(5)	The 7th house from Venus falls in Virgo sign and aspected by Mars.	The 7th house from Venus falls in Gemini Sign and tenanted by Saturn.	3	In case of boy the aspect of Venus over *Bhagyasthana* is an asset of this horoscopes. In case of girl the 7th house from Venus afflicted due to placement of Saturn. Saturn delay in matter she has not got any status so far however this Saturn will provide her a good job in due course of time. Further she may not derive full satisfaction of married life though Saturn is *rajyogkarka* yet first rate natural malefic. Here matching is not satisfactory.

(6)	The last but not the least part in overall influence on the 7th house. In case of boy the 7th house is not aspected by any planet.	In case of girl too the 7th house is not aspe-cited by any planet.	0	This renders both the horoscopes fairly weak as far as married life is concerned. From both the charts it can be deducted that their married life will be just normal neither partners drawing any inspiration from each others. Therefore at this point horoscopes must not get full point.
		Total	25	

As per classical way of matching of both the charts 25 points have been obtained. According to this method too 25 points have been obtained. This new method of matching at least point out the weak point of horoscope as far as married life is concerned.

Boy: DOB 14/15.12.1970 born at Agra at 3.40 a.m.
Girl: DOB 23.10.1973 born at Agra (U.P.) at 10:00 a.m.

Natal Chart of Boy

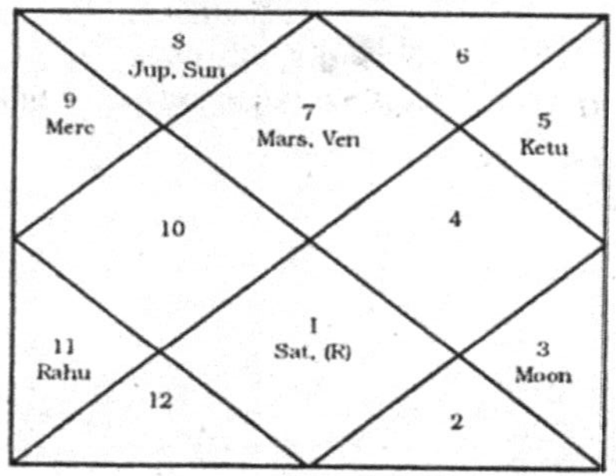

Natal Chart of Girl

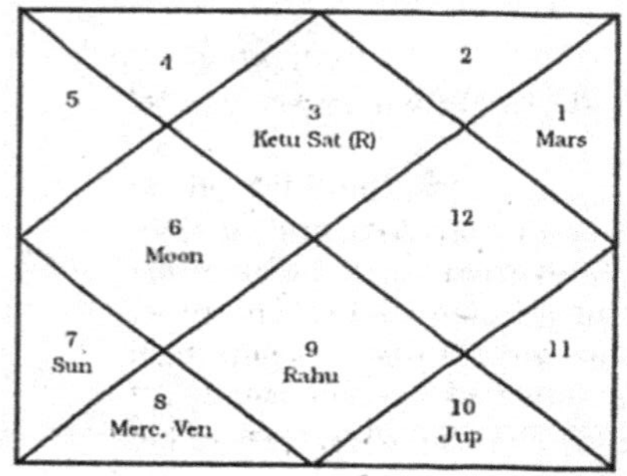

MATCHING OF CHARTS

	Boy	Girl	Points	Reason
1.	The Lagna falls in Libra sign ruled by Venus. The Rajyogakarka for this Lagana Saturn. Mars Venus are placed in Lagna.	The Lagna falls in Gemini sign ruled by Mercury. The Rajyogakarka for this Lagna is Venus Saturn is placed in Lagna.	3	Since the rulers of both the Lagna are friendly to each other. However in case of boy the placement of Mars-Venus in Lagna makes the native lustful. The placement of Mars with Venus reduces the good effect of Malaya yoga. In case of girl the placement of Saturn in Lagna makes one suffering from various ailments. Though Lana rulers are friendly toe ach other yet the placement of planets dose not allow the horoscopes to get full points.
2.	The 7th house is ruled by Mars and tenanted by Saturn.	The 7th house is ruled by Jupiter and tenanted by Rahu.	0	In case of boy, Mars and Saturn being natural enemy to each other influence the 7th house and the resultant effects weakens the 7th house considerably. In case of girl the 7th house is tenanted by Rahu and the ruler becomes debilitated therefore the 7th house is spoiled.
3.	The natural significator of marriage i.e. Venus is placed in Lagna with Mars (please see the note on Mars and Venus conjunction)	The Venus is placed in the 6th house along with Mercury (please see note on Venus-Mercury conjuction.	0	The sharp contradictory dispositions are present in the horoscopes. No matching.
4.	The 7th house from Moon is ruled by Jupiter which is	The 7th house from Moon is ruled by Jupiter which is	3	From sign point of view horoscopes get matched but If Jupiter is taken into

	placed in the 2nd house with the Sun.	debilitated in the 8th house.		consideration these it cannot be said to be matched horoscopes. Because in case of boy, Jupiter is placed in the 2nd house which happens to be 12th to the 7th sign counted from Moon. In case of girl the Jupiter is debilitated and placed in the 8th house therefore horoscopes get only 50% matching at this point.
5.	The 7th house from Venus falls in Aries sign.	The 7th house from Venus falls in Taurus sign.	0	Both the signs from Venus are enemy to each other.
6.	The overall influence on the 7th house shows that Saturn is placed their in and aspected by Mars-Venus.	The 7th house is occupied by Rahu and aspected by Saturn.	1 ½	In case of boy the 7th house is aspected by Lanesh and the ruler of the 7th house. The placement of Saturn is not at all desirable here though it is Rajyogkarka. However the two natural malefic influences this house. In case of girl the aspect of Saturn over the 7th house and quite unfavourable dispositions spoil this house. The horoscopes get ¼ points because the horoscopes of boys prevent the mishappenings of married life like divorce etc.
		Total	7½	

The traditional way of matching gives 25 points. The couples are different in their nature. The boy is emotionally wretched while the girl is peevish in nature. They have frequent tussle in their married life. They have no issue so far.

Learned readers may ponder over the new ways of matching.

The matching of charts has been done with those points which are prevalent in northern India only.

Note: In the interpretation of chart under heading 'reason' many points have been avoided to fallacy of verbosity. Readers are requested to consult the preface of this article.